hamlyn

JUNIOR GOLF

NICK WRIGHT
FOREWORD BY COLIN MONTGOMERIE

GOLF
FOUNDATION

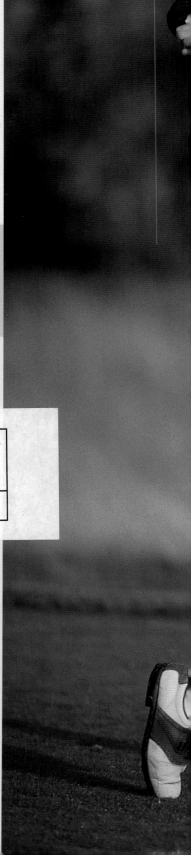

ACKNOWLEDGEMENTS

A lot of work goes on behind the scenes to produce a book like this and the project requires the co-operation and assistance from a number of people. Firstly, a huge thank you to The London Club, in Kent, England, for allowing us to shoot the photos for this book on their wonderful two courses, for making us feel so welcome during our three days on site and for the constant supply of bacon sandwiches and coffee.

Thanks also to Callaway Golf, for supplying the golf clubs for the studio photography, Stuart Dowsett, the club professional at Ilford Golf Club, and Gavin Ryan, head professional at The London Club, for their advice and input on the photo shoots and also for their consultancy work during the writing of the text.

And last, but certainly not least, a massive thank you to all of the young golfers who gave up their Saturday and Sunday morning rounds of golf to pose for the pictures, for their enthusiasm, co-operation and exemplary behaviour. If all young golfers are like this, then the future of the game is in very safe hands indeed.

PUBLISHER'S NOTE

On the majority of occasions players have been referred to as 'he' in the book.
This is simply for convenience and in no way reflects an opinion that golf is a male-only sport.
The text has been written from the point-of-view of teaching a right-handed player. Reverse the advice given for left-handed players to read 'left' for 'right' and vice versa.

Executive Editor: **Julian Brown**
Senior Editor: **Trevor Davies**
Creative Director: **Keith Martin**
Executive Art Editor: **Geoff Fennell**
Design: **Martin Topping**
Illustration: **David Beswick**
Picture Research: **Liz Fowler**
Production Controller: **Sarah Scanlon**

First published in Great Britain in 2000
by Hamlyn, an imprint of Octopus Publishing Group Limited
2–4 Heron Quays, London E14 4JP

First published in paperback 2002

Copyright © 2000, 2002 Octopus Publishing Group Limited

ISBN 0 600 60443 8

A catalogue record for this book is available from the British Library

Produced by Toppan
Printed in China

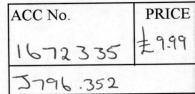

FOREWORD

Looking back over my career as a professional golfer during the past 13 years, I have to admit that the game of golf has been very good indeed to me and my family. I've had the opportunity to visit all four corners of the globe, play on some of the world's most challenging courses, meet lots of wonderful people and make plenty of new friends along the way. From a personal performance perspective, I'd like to think that I've been reasonably successful, too. I'm obviously very proud indeed to have topped the PGA European Tour Order of Merit for the past seven seasons and to have represented not only my country in the Alfred Dunhill and World Cup of Golf, but also Europe in some titanic Ryder Cup encounters against the Americans. Those of you who have followed my career will also know that I've been right there in the thick of it in several Major Championships and although things haven't quite gone my way when it matters most, I can honestly say that I've enjoyed every single minute – well, almost every minute!

Although I sincerely hope and believe that the best years of my career are yet to come, if I had to stop playing golf tomorrow, I would still have enough fantastic memories and experiences to last me a lifetime. The funny thing is, though, that when I cast my mind back over my golfing career and think about all the great experiences I've enjoyed in recent years, I still fondly recall my early carefree youth. People often say that your schooldays are the best of your life and I must admit that I agree with every word. It's not until you become an adult and undertake responsibilities and commitments, such as work, family and a mortgage, that you fully appreciate the freedom of your youth. My advice to young players right now is to make the most of every single minute. Don't take your golf too seriously. Just enjoy it.

Most of the world's top golfers play for the sheer love of the game, the thrill of the competition and the desire to continually improve and test themselves against our peers and colleagues. However, all the potential Ryder Cup and Major Championship victories in the world could never come close to matching the wonderful memories I have of playing golf as a youngster with my father and brother back home in Scotland. I still fondly remember the times when my Dad would accompany me to local tournaments when I was an up-and-coming amateur and give me some little nuggets of advice about how I should go out and play the course.

Like most young golf enthusiasts, I lived for golf and would spend the whole day at the course in the school holidays. I was fortunate enough to live right next to the famous Royal Troon Golf Club, on the west coast of Scotland, where my father was the Club Secretary until recently. The light mornings and late evenings gave me ample time to fit in plenty of golf but, I could never get enough of the game.

Nowadays, opportunities for young golfers are better than ever. Teaching standards are continually improving and there are now several mini Tours which are run for juniors who want to gain an early experience of head-to-head competition. What I can't stress highly enough to juniors, though is the need to put as much effort into their school studies as they do with their golf. My parents continually stressed the importance of trying to achieve the best grades possible and it's a subject which I feel particularly strongly about, too. Professional golf is a tough way to make a living and the casualty rate is very high. I've seen too many very good golfers sacrifice their studies for their golf and have ended up working at driving ranges picking up balls when they found they couldn't make it on Tour. If you have a good education to fall back on, you'll still be able to make a career for yourself.

Other than that, I have no hesitation whatsoever in recommending any youngster to try his or her hand at golf. It's a healthy way to spend a few hours and the friendships you make while growing up will last a lifetime.
Indeed, nothing gives me greater pleasure than seeing a group of youngsters enjoying a casual round of golf on the course, laughing, joking among each other and having fun. That's what life's all about, after all, isn't it?

Colin Montgomerie

7

INTRODUCTION
FOR PARENTS AND JUNIORS

I don't know quite what it is about being 14 years old, but it's a time when several of the world's top players claim to have first shown an interest in golf. Britain's greatest ever player, Nick Faldo, was a 14-year-old school-boy when he sat up with his father on a Sunday evening and watched the game's greatest ever player, Jack Nicklaus, win the Masters at Augusta in 1971. Fifteen years later, current young gun Lee Westwood was the exactly the same age when he, too, saw Jack win the Masters – this time in 1986.

Likewise, my first memory of golf is watching a blonde-haired American named Bill Rogers stroll to victory in the Open over the challenging links of Royal St Georges, in 1981 when I was – yes, you've guessed it – just 14 years old.

That, however, is where the similarities sadly end. Unlike Westwood and Faldo, who were inspired to greatness by the sight of the blossoming azaeleas, immaculate fairways and lightning fast greens of the famous Augusta National golf course, I have to admit that, at the time, I actually found golf rather boring. Instead of pestering my Dad to take me straight over to the nearest golf course, all I can remember is imploring him to switch channels because there was something infinitely more interesting on the other side.

However, it wasn't too long before I finally got bitten by the golf bug. My Dad would often take me over to the local public course for nine holes on a Sunday evening and I remember taking more than my fair share of air shots while watching in total awe as my Dad actually managed to make some kind of half-decent contact with the ball. I was particularly impressed by the way he managed to achieve such a low, piercing trajectory with every club in the bag. It wasn't until several years later that I discovered that this was called 'topping' the ball!

Blissfully unaware of the need for a series of starter lessons, I learnt to play by watching my Dad which, as anyone who has seen him swing a club will agree, probably wasn't the most sensible way to initiate a career in golf. With the benefit of hindsight, I now know that this is where it all started to go wrong. At the time, instead of familiarising myself with the basics of the game – the grip, address position and alignment – all I was interested in was getting out on the course with my friends. Playing virtually every day during the school holidays and at weekends enabled me to progress to about a 10 handicap by the time I was 16 years old, but then I hit a brick wall. Try as I might, I just couldn't get any better.

Reluctantly, as a very last resort, I approached a local pro for a lesson. Thinking that my swing was a vision to behold, I was staggered to discover on video that I had a bad grip, a sloppy posture and even worse alignment. He was amazed that I could break 100, let alone dip below 80 every now and then! The pro – Stuart Dowsett who you will find helping out some of the young golfers in this book – stressed that in order to achieve my goal of becoming a scratch golfer I would have to re-vamp my whole address position. How I wish I had taken his advice. Despite several years of continual work on my game, my old habits still come back to haunt me today.

The moral of the story is that, as a parent, you will obviously be very influential in your child's development as a golfer. Your son or daughter will instinctively try to copy you, so unless you are a proficient player yourself it's best to leave the real teaching to the professionals. However, your children will spend most of their golfing time in your company, so it will be helpful for you to know the basics of the game as and when you are required to help out.

As the Instruction Editor of *Golf Monthly*, I've been fortunate enough to have picked the brains of many of the world's top players and finest coaches. The one thing I've learnt from them is how importantly they view the basics. The top players review their grip, stance, alignment and posture on virtually a daily basis because they know that if something goes wrong with their swing on the course, the chances are it can be traced back to a flaw at the set-up stage.

If you take just one thing from this book, make sure that it's the importance of constantly encouraging your child to master the basic fundamentals of the game. It makes learning the more advanced techniques a whole lot easier and will save you both a lot of frustration – not to mention expensive 'corrective' lessons – at a later date.

This book is designed to help you teach children to play in conjunction with a PGA qualified professional. You won't find any in-depth technical analysis – again that's best left to the pros – but what you will find is a gentle introduction to all the key areas of the game which you can use as a reference when helping your child develop his or her skills.

Fortunately, helping youngsters take their first steps in golf has never been easier. Junior golf is currently enjoying an unprecedented boom period. Tiger Woods and Sergio Garcia on the men's Tour and Se Ri Pak and the teenage Wongluekiet twins from Thailand on the Ladies Tour have shown the world that you don't have to wait until you're 30 or 40 to play your best golf. Golf associations around the world are recognizing the importance of encouraging young talent. In the UK, the Golf Foundation, through it specialist learning programmes and initiatives, is dedicated to bringing more and more talented youngsters into the game. Meanwhile, the standard of coaching continues to improve, while equipment companies and the media are also beginning to appreciate that the junior golfer of today will be the consumer with disposable income of tomorrow.

So what are you waiting for? Enjoy the game, enjoy the book and have a lot of fun on the golf course.

Nick Wright

ALL ABOUT GOLF

Junior players are full of enthusiasm and, in most cases, can't wait to get out onto the course with their parents or friends to test out their swing. They will also be keen to find out exactly why everyone who takes up golf soon gets completely and utterly hooked on it. But before slipping off shoes and stepping into spikes, young players need a little background information about the game. They will need to know how to keep score, what equipment is needed, what types of games there are, and some of the basic rules and etiquette.

In this chapter, you can find all the information that your golfing protégé will need to get started in this most challenging of sports. There is also a wealth of background material about the traditions of golf, the top tournaments and the best players.

1

WHAT IS GOLF?

Although you can play on your own, golf is normally enjoyed by a group of two, three or four people playing on a large area of land called a golf course. Most courses comprise 18 holes of different lengths and varied difficulty, although some smaller courses only have nine holes. The game's objective is to hit the ball, using one of a range of clubs, from the teeing area at the start of the hole into the small hole on the green in the fewest number of strokes.

To test the golfer's skills, the course designer will have placed various hazards, such as bunkers, areas of long grass (rough), lakes and ditches, on each hole. The golfer must avoid hitting his ball into these hazards, as doing so will result in a more difficult next shot, or even penalty shots. As a result, golf is a game that requires patience, strategic thinking, well-honed analytical skills, good hand-eye co-ordination and athletic ability.

Unlike many other sports, which are played on the same type of court every time, one of the major attractions of golf is that no two courses are exactly the same. Golf is played on a wide variety of terrain. Parkland, heathland, woodland and seaside (links) are four of the most common settings.

WHERE TO PLAY

A budding golfer has two options open to him: he can either play at a public course or join a private members' club. On most public courses, anyone can turn up on the day and play, although at some of the more modern public courses, which operate booking systems, players have to reserve their tee-times in advance. The advantages of playing on a public course are that you don't need an official handicap and, most significantly, you don't have to pay annual subscriptions or membership fees. In other words, you only pay when you play.

To become a member of a private club, players must apply in writing to the Club Secretary or the club's committee. More clubs are now actively seeking junior players in their own right, but, junior applications are still more likely to be approved if one or both of the child's parents are already members of the club.

Joining a private club enables golfers to obtain a handicap certificate, which indicates a player's standard of play. Once a player has a handicap, he can enter club competitions, and play with and against golfers of different ages and abilities.

For those who intend to play a lot of golf at weekends and during school holidays, joining a private or semi-private club is usually the most cost-effective option. Private clubs traditionally charge an annual subscription fee that, within reason, allows the player to play as often as he wants. Semi-private clubs, which combine a standard membership structure with daily green fees, give the best of both worlds.

Finally, one very important piece of advice: young players should only join private clubs that actively support junior golf. Sadly, even today, there are still a few clubs around that are intolerant towards juniors, and provide them with very little access to the golf course. Thankfully, as more youngsters take up the game, such stuffy clubs are becoming more of a rarity, but they are still around, so watch out for them.

Above: The testing seaside links of Royal St George's regularly hosts the Open Championship.

Left: Noblethorpe Hall is a fine example of an established parkland golf course.

THE HANDICAP SYSTEM

The handicapping system, which is administered by every golf club in the country via the English Golf Union (EGU), enables players of differing abilities to compete against each other on an equal footing. A handicap is an indicator of a player's ability, and is initially calculated by taking the average score over three rounds. It is then adjusted after every competitive round played.

A golfer with an 18 handicap, for example, is expected to take 90 shots to complete a par-72 course, while a 10-handicapper will expect to play 82 shots on the same course. Therefore, the two golfers can compete against each other by deducting their respective handicaps from their final score.

Another important benefit of an official club handicap is that it enables players to play at other private clubs. A handicap is proof that a player is an established golfer with a good knowledge of the game's rules and etiquette. Players who are in possession of a handicap certificate will normally be welcome visitors at most golf clubs.

WHAT IS PAR?

Par is the recommended number of strokes it should take an expert golfer (for example, a professional) to complete a hole. You'll find a mixture of three types of holes on a golf course: par-3s, par-4s and par-5s. On a par-3, for example, players are expected to hit one shot onto the green, followed by two putts. On a par-4, they are expected to hit a tee shot, followed by an approach shot onto the green, followed by two putts. On par-5s players have the luxury of being able to play three shots to the green before taking two putts. These 'expected' routes to the hole are known as 'regulation pars', but it doesn't really matter whether a player makes par in the recommended way or whether he has to scramble for it. It's not 'how', but 'how many'.

POPULAR METHODS OF SCORING

MEDAL

The medal system, which is also known as stroke play, is the purest form of individual scoring as every single shot counts. A player's score at the end of the round is the number of shots played minus his handicap. This calculation gives you the 'net score'.

STABLEFORD

Under the Stableford method, players score points for bogeys, pars, birdies, eagles and better. The advantage of this system, is that because points can be scored on each hole, players are able to make up for poor starts and, therefore, matches often stay competitive right down to the last hole.

A player with a handicap of zero (often called a scratch player), will score Stableford points as follows:

Bogey = 1 point
Par = 2 points
Birdie = 3 points
Eagle = 4 points
Albatross = 5 points

The situation is, however, more complicated for players who have a handicap of one or more. In such cases, the player's handicap is translated into extra shots, so a 12-handicapper will be given one extra shot on each of the 12 most difficult holes (as determined by the course's stroke index). In this way, a score of seven on a difficult par-5 will still score one point (for a net bogey).

MATCHPLAY

Matchplay is the most traditional form of competitive golf. Instead of amassing points per hole or counting the number of shots played during a round, you play for holes instead. Whoever takes the fewest shots wins the hole. The winner is the player who wins the most holes during the round.

DATE _____

COMPETITION _____

PLAYER A _____   HANDICAP _____   STROKES _____

PLAYER B _____   HANDICAP _____   STROKES _____

Hole	Champ.	Men	Ladies	Par	Stroke Index	Gross Score A	B	Net Score A	B
1	390	345	320	4	11				
2	500	470	415	5	3				
3	387	350	285	4	7				
4	171	135	110	3	17				
5	505	480	435	5	1				
6	350	315	290	4	13				
7	182	160	142	3	15				
8	385	350	320	4	5				
9	355	320	290	4	9				
OUT	3225	2925	2607	36					

❶   ❷   ❸ ❹ ❺ ❻

Hole	Champ.	Men	Ladies	Par	Stroke Index	Gross Score A	B	Net Score A	B
10	410	375	340	4	2				
11	190	160	112	3	18				
12	460	425	380	5	8				
13	325	285	255	4	12				
14	383	350	300	4	10				
15	200	160	125	3	14				
16	372	330	270	4	16				
17	510	490	465	5	4				
18	413	370	338	4	6				
IN	3263	2945	2585	36					
OUT	3225	2925	2607	36					
TOTAL	6488	5870	5192	72					
						HANDICAP			
						NET SCORE			

PLAYER'S SIGNATURE _____ ←❼

❶ **Distance** – This column indicates the length of each hole in yards.

❷ **Tees** – Most golf clubs have a variety of tees to play from. The red tees are for ladies, yellow tees are usually for non-competitive rounds, while the white tees are usually reserved for club competitions.

❸ **Stroke index** – This column indicates the relative difficulty of the hole. Stroke index one is deemed to be the most difficult hole on the course, stroke index 18 is deemed to be the easiest.

❹ **Your score** – Keep a record of your own score in this column.

❺ **Partner's score** – Mark your playing partner's score here

❻ **Net score** – A player's net score is his actual score minus his handicap.

❼ **Signature** – A player should always check his score very carefully before signing a scorecard. Although in competitions, someone else will be marking your card, it is your responsibility to make sure that the information recorded is correct. Once a player has put his signature on the bottom of the card, the score stands.

FILLING IN A SCORECARD

When players check in at the pro-shop or clubhouse to pay their green fees, they will be given a scorecard. The cards give information on each hole and have space to fill in at least two players' scores. When playing in competitions, players are not allowed to mark their own cards. Each player must swap scorecards with someone else in their group before starting.

THE HISTORY AND ORIGINS OF GOLF

Although both the Scots and the Dutch enthusiastically claim to have invented the game in Europe, the precise origins of golf remain unclear, despite much historical research. The famous St Andrews golf course, in Fife, Scotland, is known throughout the world as 'the home of golf', but there is plenty of evidence to suggest that forms of a game involving a stick, a ball and a hole have been played all around the globe for well over 700 years.

It is not surprising that the game has existed for so long, because golf is essentially a very simple game. In the early days, the equipment was simple, too. Golf clubs were made from hickory shafts, which were attached to large metal heads, and golf balls were fashioned from the skins of dead animals sewn together and stuffed with feathers or pieces of cloth. It's all a far cry from the computer-designed, aerodynamic golf balls and graphite clubs of the 21st century. However, if you find any of these old clubs lying around in your garage or attic, don't throw them away. Collecting golf memorabilia is extremely popular, and authentic old clubs can fetch six-figure sums at auction.

In the early days of competitive golf in the middle of the 19th century, many of the best players of the day were club-makers. Willie Park Snr. won the first Open Championship at Prestwick in 1860 using clubs that he had put together in his own workshop. It's difficult to imagine Tiger Woods or David Duval doing the same today.

In the very early days of professional golf, the top players, such as Alex Herd, James Braid, J.W. Taylor and Harry Vardon were clubmakers too.

PROFESSIONAL TOURS

Each year, the world's top players compete against each other in a series of tournaments, which are known collectively as a Tour. The three main Tours are: the PGA European Tour, which stages events throughout Europe; the USPGA Tour, which moves around America; and the Japanese PGA Tour. There are also several smaller Tours in Asia and Australia, as well as a series of secondary or satellite Tours, which often act as a feeder system into the main Tours. Sponsors provide the prize-money for these tournaments, and in return they receive media exposure and the prestige of being associated with the sport of golf.

Most professional tournaments are played over four days, and there is usually a halfway 'cut' after the second day. The cut trims the field from about 150 to 80 for the final two days. Players who miss the cut do not receive any prize-money.

At the end of the season, the top 125 or so players retain their right to play on the Tour the following year. This is called 'keeping your card'. Players who do not retain their Tour card have to go back to the Qualifying School, where they will compete against newcomers who are trying to progress onto the Tour for the first time.

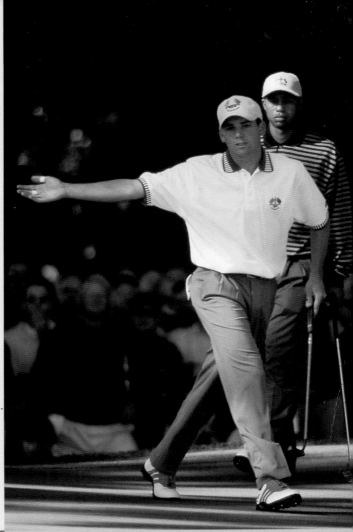

Top: America's Tiger Woods and Spain's Sergio Garcia look set to dominate golf over the next couple of decades.

Right: The Ryder Cup is arguably the most keenly contested sporting trophy in the world.

THE RYDER CUP

Named after Samuel Ryder, who in 1927 organized the first matchplay competition between Great Britain and Ireland and America, the Ryder Cup is now one of the most popular and thrilling sporting contests in the world. For the first 58 years, the American side dominated the competition (winning 21 of the first 25 Cups) so to make things even, it was decided that the Great Britain and Ireland team should be replaced with a team from all of Europe. The Ryder Cup is now held every two years, and the matches are so keenly contested that there is rarely more than a point between the two sides.

THE MAJOR CHAMPIONSHIPS

Although professionals rely on the prize-money that they earn from Tour events to make a living, their careers and status in the history of the game are judged not on their bank balances, but on their performances in the game's four Major Championships: The Masters, The US Open, The Open and the USPGA Championship.

Each of these prestigious tournaments has a rich history, and they are undoubtedly the events that the players want to win most. The Majors are all played on tough, uncompromising golf courses, and test not only the player's technical ability, but also his mental resilience under the severest of pressure. Players such as Nick Faldo and Tiger Woods organize their schedules around these four championships and all their preparation work is geared accordingly.

Winning a Major brings not only status but also increased earning power. Although the prize-money is often less than that on offer at other Tour events, because of the global recognition a player achieves by winning a Major, the victory is worth a fortune in terms of lucrative endorsements and sponsorships.

Jack Nicklaus is widely regarded as the game's greatest ever player because of his unparalleled record in the Major Championships. His tally of 20 Major wins is 11 more than his nearest challenger, Gary Player.

THE MASTERS

Created by the legendary Bobby Jones in 1934, The Masters Tournament, played each year in April, is unique for several reasons. Firstly, it's the only Major that is played each year on the same course – Augusta National. Secondly, although there are several ways to qualify automatically, it is essentially an invitation event. The winner receives a Green Jacket and a life-time exemption. Augusta National is renowned for its lightning fast greens and immaculate condition.

The Masters is also a very popular tounament among European players, who dominated the event in the 1990s.

Top left: America's legendary Jack Nicklaus, who has won 20 Major Championships, is widely regarded as the game's greatest ever player.

Left: Nick Faldo presents Ian Woosnam with the famous Augusta National green jacket in 1991.

THE US OPEN

The US Open is the national championship of the United States and dates back to the 19th century. A traditional US Open course has narrow fairways and very fast greens, which are flanked by collars of thick rough. Not surprisingly, many American golfers claim this to be the championship they want to win the most.

THE OPEN CHAMPIONSHIP

Easily the oldest of the four Major Championships, the Open is played on links courses. Willie Park Snr. won the first Open Championship at Prestwick in 1860. The Open, which is held each year in July, is traditionally played on courses featuring large, undulating greens and fast, running fairways with very little rough.

THE USPGA CHAMPIONSHIP

Regarded by many as the weakest of the four Majors, the USPGA started out as a matchplay event, however, a lack of interest and a succession of mediocre finalists prompted a switch to a standard strokeplay format. The USPGA is held each year in August, and is usually played in hot, humid weather. The course set-up is very similar to that of a US Open course.

Left: Such is the impact that Tiger Woods has had on the game since he turned professional in 1996 that he is the favourite for every Major Championship.

THE SOLHEIM CUP

Named after Karsten Solheim – the founder of Karsten Manufacturing (the company that makes Ping golf clubs) – the Solheim Cup is the ladies' equivalent of the Ryder Cup. It is played every two years, alternating between venues in the United States and Europe. Although the first match was only staged in 1988, as the ladies' Tours in Europe and America continue to build in strength, the Solheim Cup looks sure to become as popular and competitive as the Ryder Cup.

Right: England's Laura Davies has achieved enormous success in the game and has played in every Solheim Cup match since 1988.

GOLF ON THE INTERNET

Golf is one of the most frequently searched-for subjects on the Internet, with around 1.5 million web sites already dedicated to the sport. All that information at your fingertips sounds like bliss, but the only problem is locating sites that are informative, interesting and interactive. No doubt you'll want do your own research, but here's a selection of some of the best sites to get you started.

JUNIOR GOLF

Although often neglected by television, newspapers and magazines, information on junior golf is widely available on the Internet. There are several sites dedicated to this subject, offering handy hints and tips on joining clubs, playing in tournaments and choosing equipment.

www.juniorgolf.com
www.golf-foundation.org
www.nickfaldo.prg/faldojuniorseries
www.juniorgolftour.com

PLAYERS

Many of the world's top players now have their own web sites. Normally, these sites offer detailed profiles and biographies, transcripts from recent interviews, facts and figures and a regular column from the player. In some cases, you can even exchange e-mails with the player.

JOHN DALY
www.gripitandripit.com
DAVID DUVAL
jacksonville.com/special/fatherandson/
ERNIE ELS
www.ernieels.com
NICK FALDO
members.aol.com/ChrisDicks/Faldo.html
COLIN MONTGOMERIE
www.golfweb.com/library/playing-editors/montgomerie
JACK NICKLAUS
www.nicklaus.com
GREG NORMAN
www.golfonline.com/greatwhiteshark
LEE WESTWOOD OFFICIAL FAN CLUB
www.westyuk.com
TIGER WOODS
www.tigerwoods.com

GOLF INSTRUCTION

Nothing beats personal tuition for learning how to play golf, but there is a huge amount of instructional material available to choose from on the Internet. Many of the world's top coaches have their own official sites where you can view video clips, read instruction articles, view the swings of the world's top players frame by frame and exchange e-mails.

www.golfdigital.com
www.thegolfchannel.com
www. Leadbetterschools.com

EQUIPMENT

Most of the top manufacturers and retailers have their own web sites, so the Internet is the best way to gather information on the latest equipment trends. Many of these sites even feature interactive shopping.

EQUIPMENT AND ACCESSORIES

In the past, golf clubs and golf balls were made from very basic materials, however, nowadays manufacturers have access to a range of high-tech alloys and fibres. The materials used to make the shaft and clubhead of the latest mega driver may also be found on the heat shields of a space shuttle, or on the wings of a multi-million dollar super jet fighter. However, all this space-age technology makes choosing a set of clubs somewhat perplexing for the average junior golfer.

BUYING A STARTER SET

If you've watched the top professionals playing golf on television, you probably think that carrying a set of clubs around the golf course must be a tiring business. The caddies you see at the big tournaments carry a large golf bag, containing up to 14 clubs, together with golf balls, waterproof clothing, towels, an umbrella and various accessories. Fortunately, the average player does not have to go such extremes.

The Rules state that players can carry up to 14 clubs in their bag; however, for youngsters just starting out in the game, there's really no need to carry the full quota. Most 'starter sets' for juniors contain only five clubs: a wood, three different irons and a putter. This is certainly adequate for players to learn the basic skills of the game. Juniors can add to their set as and when they need to.

6-IRON 8-IRON PITCHING WEDGE DRIVER

IRONS

Most junior 'starter sets' contain a 6-iron, an 8-iron and a pitching wedge. Each club has a slightly different job. The higher the number on the iron, the greater the amount of loft it has on the clubface. A club with more loft will send the ball higher into the air, but it will travel less distance. Therefore, a 6-iron will hit the ball lower and further than a 9-iron, which will send the ball higher, but not very far toward the hole in comparison.

Junior clubs tend to be manufactured with a little more loft than adult clubs. This modification helps the young player to get the ball into the air more easily. It is also true to say that the more loft a club has, the easier it is to hit well, which is great for developing confidence.

WOODS

With only rare exceptions, woods aren't actually made from wood any more. Nowadays, these clubs are made from metal, which is good news for youngsters because metal heads are far lighter and, therefore, easier to swing. A junior's first wood should be a 3- or 4-wood, as these are relatively easy to hit off the tee, and they can also be used from the fairway.

As a junior develops his strength and starts to get better at the game, he will quickly need to add to his set. A driver is a good early addition to a young player's golf bag. The driver is a 'wood' used off the tee, which has very little loft because it is designed to give as much distance as possible. After that, he may want to look at filling in the gaps between the irons, perhaps going as low as a 4-iron, and adding a sand wedge, too, for playing out of bunkers and around the green.

THE ANATOMY OF A GOLF CLUB

Golf clubs are assembled from three basic components: a grip, a shaft and a clubhead. Each component has a different role to play in helping the player to strike the ball.

THE GRIP

This is where the player places his hands on the club to hold it. Grips come in a variety of different sizes and textures. It's very important to play with clubs fitted with the correct grip thickness for your hands.

THE SHAFT

The shaft connects the grip to the clubhead. Shafts are most commonly made from stainless steel, but are also available in a variety of different materials, including graphite and titanium. The shaft is the most complex of the three components, as its thickness and weight will greatly influence the shape and trajectory of shots. Shafts come in a variety of different flexibilities. Professionals and players who generate a lot of clubhead speed usually prefer to use a stiffer shaft, while higher handicappers (including most juniors who swing more slowly) should opt for more flexibility to help compensate for their lack of swing speed.

THE CLUBHEAD

The clubhead takes the full force of a golf shot, so it needs to be made from a durable material. Clubhead designs have changed considerably over the years, from a 'blade' style, where the head was forged from a flat piece of metal, to the more modern cavity-back style, which is made from a mould. Although several Tour professionals still prefer the feel and versatility of a bladed club, most professionals prefer the cavity-backed clubs, which are considered to be more user-friendly and forgiving. The grooves on the clubface are helpful for lining up the shot, but they also help to create backspin, so keep them clean.

WHY YOU SHOULD AVOID CUT-DOWN CLUBS

Equipment designed specifically for juniors has improved dramatically in recent years. Not so long ago, a child would begin playing golf with a 'cut-down' club – an adult-sized golf club that has simply been trimmed down to suit a child's height. However, cut-down clubs can often do more harm than good, as the shaft becomes much stiffer once it has been shortened, making it harder for a child to swing and hit.

Cut-down clubs are also very heavy, particularly for a small child, and the grip may well be too thick as well.

The first thing children and teenagers want to see when they hit a golf ball is it travelling through the air – that's where the fun comes in. Using a cut-down club won't be too helpful in this department and may even put a youngster off the game for good.

Thankfully, these days the cut-down has become something of a rarity. More golf club manufacturers are now making clubs specifically designed for children. To this end, lighter heads, thinner grips and more flexible shafts are used. The results are clubs that help young players have some fun with the game.

CUSTOM CLUB-FITTING – MATCHING THE CLUBS TO THE SWING

Using made-to-measure clubs is advisable for players of all ages, shapes and sizes. Custom-fitting, as the procedure is more commonly known, ensures that the clubs are suited to the particular player. With children and teenagers this means looking at two or three key areas. As mentioned earlier, the grips will need to be thinner for a junior's smaller hands and the shafts more flexible, too. But the most important consideration of all is the length of the clubs. Golf clubs that are too long or too short, encourage poor posture and are difficult to hit consistently.

Most manufacturers fit juniors by height. It's a simple process, which usually involves measuring the distance between the child's hand and the floor when they're standing normally. This measurement gives a good guide as to the length of club the child should be using. It is also important to remember that juniors can grow very quickly. Some manufacturers offer trade-in schemes, which will deflect some of the cost, but to a certain extent it is also possible to purchase equipment that the child will grow into. Most experts recommend that you shouldn't go beyond 1 inch (2.5cm) longer on a club to start with. It is also possible to lengthen an existing club by 1 inch (2.5cm) or so to cope with a growth spurt. So just because the child grows a little doesn't necessarily mean you have to buy them a new set of clubs.

WHICH GOLF BAG?

Junior golf bags are very well designed these days. They have to be robust enough to take the inevitable knocks and man-handling, but also light enough for a youngster to carry for 18 holes. Some junior bags even use a double-strap carrying system – popular with adult bags – which spreads the weight evenly across the back and shoulders. A bag with a stand is also useful, as it will keep the clubs and the bag itself reasonably clean even when playing in wet weather.

PUTTERS – WHY LOOKS ARE IMPORTANT

More than any other club in the bag, putters come in a huge variety of designs. It is also true that, because of the individual nature of this area of the game, it's difficult to recommend particular makes or styles. However, if a putter looks good to a particular player, that's half the battle. As any Tour professional will tell you, it's very difficult to hole putts with a putter that you don't like the look of.

Looks aside, the only other factor a player should consider when purchasing a putter is its length. If a putter is too short, the player will probably end up crouching or stooping over the ball, which could lead to back problems. Likewise, if a club is too long, the player will stand too upright or too far away from the ball. It all comes down to creating confidence. If a youngster is uncomfortable standing over a putt he's unlikely to hole it. The best advice for any junior is to pop down to the local pro shop or golf store, try out a few and pick one that feels good when he addresses the ball.

WHAT'S IN THE BAG?

In addition to golf clubs, players must carry several important items in their bags to help deal with a wide variety of situations on the course.

Umbrella and waterproofs
Always pack an umbrella and a waterproof suit, preferably one with a breathable lining that prevents perspiration.

Towel
A large towel is fine for keeping clubs clean in dry weather, but several smaller towels are preferable when it's raining.

Pitch fork
Used to repair indentations on the green. Alternatively, a tee peg can be used for the same job.

Ball marker
Used to mark the position of a player's ball on the green before cleaning it. Alternatively, a small coin will do the job just as well.

Pencil and scorecard
For keeping score and making notes about the round.

Glove
Right-handed players wear a glove on their left hand (right hand for left-handers) to help prevent the club from slipping.

Golf balls
Always carry enough to complete the round.

WHICH GOLF BALL?

As golfers improve their skills, they tend to develop a preference for a particular type of golf ball. As a general rule, harder golf balls tend to travel further and roll more on landing, but they can feel heavy and hard off the clubface, particularly to youngsters. Golf balls with a softer cover may feel easier to hit, but they don't travel as far and won't last as long.

For a player just starting out, the make of ball probably doesn't matter too much. Modern golf balls are very expensive, so instead of splashing out on the latest designer model, youngsters should pop along to their local pro-shop and have a rummage through the used-ball bin. They will probably get two or three times as many balls for their money. There's plenty of time to become choosy and more discerning when a golfer's skills develop.

Right: A golf glove will prevent the grip from slipping in your hands when you swing the club.

FOOTWEAR

Most children starting out in the game play in training shoes, and this is fine if they play at a public golf course or a club without strict rules on footwear. However, some sportswear companies manufacture golf shoes for juniors, and youngsters who play regularly should certainly invest in such specialist footwear. Golf shoes are designed not only to be comfortable but also to give a stable footing when hitting the ball – most golf shoes are fitted with spikes that grip the ground as you swing.

Spikes are normally made from metal, but with many golf clubs now operating a soft-spike only policy, the days of the standard metal spike could well be numbered. Soft spikes are green-keeper friendly because they do not leave indentations like metal spikes. The good news is that soft spikes are also very comfortable, particularly in the summer when the fairways can be dry and hard. The one disadvantage of soft spikes is that many golfers claim they don't grip as well as traditional spikes in wet weather.

Most young players will have just one pair of shoes, so it is essential that they opt for ones that are both waterproof and lightweight. Waterproof shoes are a must during the winter, but junior players must also consider the fact that their footwear must also be light enough to wear comfortably during the warmer months of the year.

TIPS FOR PARENTS

1. Don't spend too much money too soon. Check that your child has a real liking for the game.
2. Cut-down clubs are a waste of money. Ask an expert for advice on proper junior clubs made to fit the player's height and swing characteristics.
3. Don't overburden young players with too many clubs.
   A half set of four or five irons is plenty. Add more clubs as the player's game develops.
4. Sign a beginner up for junior lessons at a local club. It's a great introduction to the game, and the teacher will usually have clubs available to use at first.
5. Don't be afraid to ask for advice from experts.
6. The more fun the player has, the more he will want to play and improve.

10 KEY RULES

Throughout the UK and Europe, the Rules of Golf are regulated by The Royal and Ancient Golf Club of St Andrews, Scotland. In the USA, the Rules are administered by the United States Golf Association (USGA). In total, there are 34 different rules, each with a variety of different applications. The Rules are comprehensive and often complex, so much so that not even the world's top players know each and every single working application. But although players need a sound knowledge of the Rules to play competitively, while learning the game they can get away with the basics. Here are ten basic rules that players need to be aware of to enjoy the game.

1. FURTHEST FROM THE HOLE PLAYS FIRST

One of the most important rules in golf is that the furthest away from the hole always plays first. This is safer for everyone involved and speeds up play.

2. WHO HAS THE HONOUR?

On the first tee in a competition round, players should flip a coin to see who plays first. After that, the player who records the best score on the first hole has the right to tee off first at the second. This is known as the honour and a player will retain it until one of his playing partners records a lower score on a hole.

3. WHERE TO TEE THE BALL UP

At the start of each hole, players must tee off from the designated teeing ground, a rectangular area two club lengths deep, the front and sides of which are outlined by two tee markers. It's important to remember that players are allowed to stand outside the teeing ground to play their shot as long as their ball is within the designated area.

4. IDENTIFYING YOUR BALL

Players must be able to identify their golf ball at any given time on the golf course, particularly if it lands in a hazard. Simply remembering the make and number is not enough. Just because a player finds a Titleist Professional 4, for example, under a tree does not make it his ball.

The first thing a Tour professional will do after opening a new pack of golf balls is to put his own identification on each one with a permanent ink marker pen. Many players write their initials under the logo, others use coloured dots or lines. The American player Duffy Waldorf gets his children to draw funny shapes all over his golf balls. It doesn't matter how a player chooses to mark his own golf balls, just so long as he can identify them clearly at a later stage.

5. WHEN TO ATTEND THE FLAG

All players must know when to leave the flag in and when to take it out of the hole. Failure to understand this rule incurs a two-shot penalty in strokeplay competition and loss of hole under matchplay. From off the green, players have the option of leaving the flag in or taking it out of the hole completely. If a player is actually on the green itself, though, he can have the flag removed or ask for it to be attended. This means that one of the other players or a caddie holds the flag while the player putts, only removing the flag as the ball nears the hole. Players are not allowed to leave the flag in the hole without it being attended when putting on the green.

6. HAZARDS

Golf course designers place a variety of hazards on the golf course to catch players out. The most penal of these are lakes and ditches, from which it is often impossible for players to retrieve their balls. There are two varieties of water hazards: normal water hazards and lateral water hazards.

   Lateral hazards are indicated by red marker posts. If a player's ball lands in a lateral hazard, he has two options. He can either play the ball from where it lies (but without grounding his club first), or he can drop a ball within two club lengths of the hazard, at the point at which the ball is judged to have first crossed the border of the hazard. However, players are not allowed to drop the ball nearer to the hole.

   If a player's ball lands in a regular water hazard, indicated by yellow marker posts, he has two options. He can either replay his shot from the same place, after first adding a stroke to his score, or he can drop the ball on a line between the point at which the ball first crossed over the border of the hazard (not necessarily where it finished) and the hole. The player may drop the ball as far back as he wants on that line.

7. OUT OF BOUNDS

In addition to normal hazards such as lakes, ditches and bunkers, a golf club may designate various areas of the course as 'out of bounds'. Play is prohibited from out of bounds areas, which are indicated by a succession of white marker posts. Players are not even allowed to enter these areas to look for or retrieve a lost ball, although they may stand out of bounds to play a ball that is lying within bounds. If a player's ball lands out of bounds, he incurs a penalty shot and then has to replay his shot from as close as possible to where he struck his first ball. You may have heard TV commentators say: 'He's playing three off the tee.' This means that a player has driven the ball out of bounds and has been penalized a shot. Therefore, his next tee shot will be his third stroke on the hole.

8. PLAYING A PROVISIONAL BALL

There are occasions when a player is unsure as to whether his ball is lost, is in a hazard or is out of bounds. In such cases, it is a good idea for the player to play a provisional ball. This enables the player to look for his first ball and then, if he can't find it, continue with his second one after adding a penalty stroke for the lost ball. This common sense approach prevents a player, who can't find his original ball, from having to walk all the way back to the tee to replay his shot. Players must, however, remember to tell their playing partners that they are playing a provisional ball before hitting the shot.

9. MARKING A BALL ON THE GREEN

Once a player reaches the green, he is allowed to pick his ball up, clean it and replace it. Before he can do that, though, he must mark his ball so that he can return it to exactly the same place. The Rules of Golf allows a player to mark his ball with any kind of object, such as a tee peg or the end of a putter, but most golfers use either a ball-marker or a coin. The correct procedure is to place the marker as close as possible behind the ball without touching it. After cleaning the ball, it must be replaced as close as possible to the marker.

10. NUMBER OF CLUBS

The Rules of Golf permit each player to carry up to 14 golf clubs in their bag during a round of golf. This means, players are limited to an initial selection, although they can replace clubs broken or deemed unfit for play during a round, providing the replacement of these clubs does not cause unnecessary delay. The penalty for carrying too many golf clubs is two strokes for each hole during which the rules were broken, up to a maximum of four strokes in a round. In matchplay the penalty is the loss of the hole for each time the rule is broken, up to a maximum of a two-hole penalty.

UNDERSTANDING ETIQUETTE

In addition to golf's complex system of rules, the game also has its own, unwritten code of behaviour known as etiquette. Sportsmanship and respect for playing partners are integral parts of the tradition and history of the game. So if you want to be taken seriously as a golfer, knowing how to conduct yourself on the course is just as important as playing good shots. Here is a selection of the most common examples of good etiquette.

ALWAYS REPAIR PITCHMARKS ON THE GREEN

When the ball lands on the green, it normally leaves an indentation known as a pitchmark. If you watch a golf tournament on television, you'll notice that the first thing professionals do as they walk onto the green is mark their ball, then look for and repair their pitchmark. It's a habit for the top players, and it's one that junior players should copy. Pitchmarks not only look unsightly but also prevent the ball from rolling smoothly on the green. In the long term, pitchmarks can permanently damage the putting surface.

To repair a pitchmark correctly, the player should use a pitchfork. Alternatively, a tee peg will suffice. The pitchfork is inserted into the green on both sides of the indentation and is used to pinch the turf inwards. Players should not raise the turf with a pitchfork, as it does more harm than good. Once the player has squeezed the turf together from all sides, he should tap down any raised grass with a putter.

LEAVE BUNKERS AS YOU EXPECT TO FIND THEM

For a golfer, there's only one sight worse than seeing your ball disappear into a bunker, and that's finding your ball lying right in the middle of an old, scruffy footprint inside a bunker. It only takes a few seconds for a player to rake a bunker once he has played his shot, but it makes a huge difference to the next person unfortunate enough to visit the sand if the bunker is left neat and tidy. Junior players should be encouraged to leave bunkers as they would expect to find them.

There is an art to raking a bunker correctly. Firstly, players should enter and exit the bunker at its lowest point, as this will avoid displacing too much sand. Secondly, the sand must be spread evenly throughout the bunker – under no circumstances should it all be raked into one place. And finally, once a player has finished raking a bunker, he must consider where to leave the rake. Different clubs have different rules, but the general recommendation is that players should leave rakes just inside the bunker, not outside where it might prevent a ball from entering the hazard.

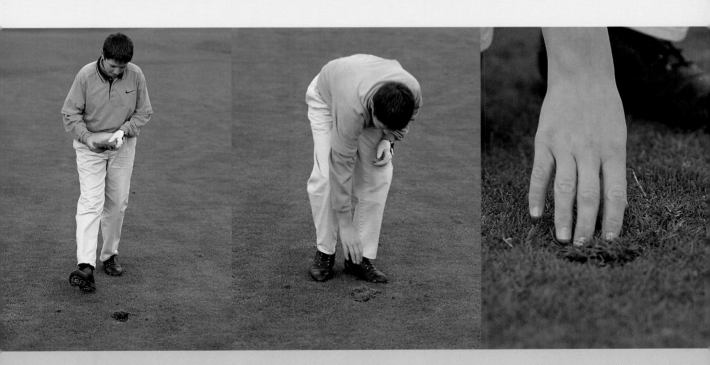

ALWAYS REPLACE DIVOTS

Golf can be an extremely frustrating game, and never more so than when a perfectly good shot ends up in a divot. The Rules state that in this situation the ball has to be played from where it lies, so there is no relief – no matter how unfair it seems. In effect, the player is punished for someone else's ignorance of etiquette.

If a player takes a divot (which he should do with most iron shots), he should also take the time to pick it up and replace it in the ground. That way, the turf is given a chance to grow back and fellow players are given the best chance of getting a good, clean lie on the fairway. The only time that a player should not replace a divot is on the tee.

REMOVE YOUR CAP BEFORE SHAKING HANDS

At the end of a round it is customary for golfers to shake hands with their playing partners. Regardless of whether a player has won or lost, he should remove his cap or headwear before offering his hand to a fellow player. This sporting gesture is essentially a sign of respect to your opponent. Many golf clubs also request that players remove headwear before entering the clubhouse.

AVOID STEPPING ON YOUR PARTNER'S PUTTING LINE

Players should always take great care not to tread on an opponent's putting line to the hole. Footprints can easily make an indentation in the green or, even worse, leave a spike mark right on the line of the putt. Ideally, players should walk either around or behind an opponent's ball to reach their own. If that's not possible, they should step carefully over the line without touching it with their feet.

NEVER TALK WHILE SOMEONE IS PLAYING A SHOT

Golf is a sport that is difficult enough without players disturbing each other's concentration by talking as a shot is about to be played. Friendly chit-chat is a central part of a social round of golf, but players must remember to stop talking when another is preparing to play a shot. In fact, players should take great care not to make any kind of noise at all. Rummaging around in a bag or jingling coins can be both off-putting and annoying.

WHERE TO STAND ON THE TEE AND ON THE FAIRWAY

For reasons of safety and etiquette, it's very important that players know exactly where to stand when someone else is playing a shot. This is particularly the case on the tee, where there can be up to four players in close proximity. The basic rule of thumb here is that players should stand level with the ball behind the player or at a slight angle behind the ball. It's bad etiquette – and dangerous – to stand ahead of the ball, in the player's eye line or directly behind the line, too. The same approach should also be adopted on the fairway. It is certainly bad form to stand directly behind someone while they're playing, and it is equally unacceptable to stand so close that you interfere with a player's line of vision.

CALL PLAYERS THROUGH WHEN LOOKING FOR A BALL

Everyone hits the ball into the trees occasionally – some more than others, of course. However, when rooting around in the bushes and the woods, players should remember to call the group behind 'through'.

Players are allowed five minutes to look for a ball, but this doesn't mean the group behind has to wait that long. If a player's looking for a ball is holding up play, wave the next group through.

ETIQUETTE

Remind juniors that they should always ...

... arrive on the first tee in plenty of time for their match

... wish their playing partners good luck at the start
of the round

... look out for their playing partner's golf ball

... shout 'fore' if their ball is in danger of hitting anyone

... replace divots (except on the tee)

... repair pitchmarks on the green

... leave their bag or trolley as close as possible
to the next tee, but not on the green

... call the group behind through if looking for a ball

... take care not to damage the course with
practice swings

Remind juniors that they should never ...

... play a shot while others in front are still in range

... talk while someone is preparing to play a shot

... stand directly behind someone when they're putting

... shout or swear on the golf course

... throw clubs or equipment in temper

... replace divots on the tee

... mark their own card on the green

... laugh at another player's misfortune

... make practice swings without making sure
they have room

... walk across someone's putting line on the green

PRACTICAL ADVICE FOR PARENTS

Children may have regular lessons from a golf professional, but they will probably spend more time playing golf in their parent's company, so it is important that mums and dads neither downplay nor underestimate their influence as teacher and role model. It is the parents who will usually explain the finer points of the rules, etiquette and behaviour. It is parents who must show their children how to fill in a scorecard correctly, and it is they who must explain which clothes and behaviour are suitable for the course and the clubhouse. The bulk of a child's golfing education will undoubtedly fall squarely on the shoulders of mum and dad.

THE RIGHT AGE TO START

When it comes to the question of what is the best age to introduce a child to golf, opinions vary as much as hair styles. Tiger Woods, for example, started to show a talent for the game when he was just 18 months old, and he was already a competent player by the time he reached school age. By contrast, Lee Westwood and Nick Faldo didn't take up the sport until they were in their early teens.

There is no age that is best to start playing golf but, in general, sooner is preferable to later. The most important thing parents can do is give their child the opportunity to play the game as soon as he shows an obvious interest. If parents are keen golfers themselves and practise regularly at home or watch the game on television, it's likely that their children will quickly become curious and will want to join in and play too.

Some children, for example, start hitting shots in the garden with a lightweight plastic club when they are as young as two. Clearly, at this age, children have no concept of the swing, but are merely enjoying swinging at the ball as hard as they can. Youngsters will often miss the ball completely, but in most cases they will be unperturbed by a succession of air shots, and will simply stand up and have another go. At this stage, the most important thing is that the child is having fun.

Even in the pre-school years, it is possible to teach youngsters the basics of grip and stance. If children have the physical dexterity to walk, play with toys and climb stairs, there's no reason why they can't learn the comparatively simple tasks of holding a golf club and standing to the ball correctly. However, when teaching children the fundamentals of the game, you should remember that good habits last a lifetime, but if left unchecked, bad habits can too.

HOW TO GET STARTED IN GOLF

LEARN THE SHORT GAME FIRST

It is no coincidence that many of the world's finest chippers and putters – players such as Sergio Garcia, Seve Ballesteros and Jose Maria Olazabal – took up the game at a very young age. A five- or six-year-old will obviously struggle to hit the ball a long way, so start with the basics of chipping and putting instead. Short-game skills will stay with players throughout their lives. Just look at Seve Ballesteros. Although Seve's driving and iron play continues to frustrate him, he was still ranked as the best putter on the PGA European Tour in 1999 and he was also in the top-10 for bunker play.

Junior players should work hard to hone their short game for two reasons. Firstly, a good short game will help young players compensate for the inevitable long-game weaknesses that they encounter as they grow and as they learn the game. Secondly, players who master the subtle skills of chipping, pitching and putting at a young age, will have the platform from which to post some really low scores once they become consistent from tee to green.

LEAVE THE TEACHING TO A PROFESSIONAL

Although demonstrating the basic fundamentals of the grip, stance, alignment and posture can usually be satisfactorily accomplished using a book or video as a guideline, such advice should ideally be provided by a qualified PGA professional. Except in the case of very low handicappers or professional golfers themselves, it's probably not a good idea to teach one's own children. That may sound a little harsh, but would you take flying or driving lessons from somebody who only knew the basics themselves? Of course not, so that's why you should leave golf lessons to the experts too.

Of course, there is nothing wrong with a little friendly parental advice every now and then, but it is very important that your input should complement that being given by the professional. Conflicting advice will not only confuse the child, it could also damage their confidence and impede their future progress in the game. Knowing when to hand over the reigns is a key to your child's golfing development.

GROUP LESSONS

A series of golf lessons can be a sizeable investment, and there aren't even any guarantees that children will actually want to take up the game. One way to ease the initial financial burden is for parents to book their children group lessons at first. Many council-run golf courses offer weekly group sessions on a Saturday or Sunday morning, and some also offer courses during the school holidays. In some instances, trial clubs are provided, so parents can avoid paying out for costly equipment until they are sure that their children want to take up the game seriously.

Group lessons are cheaper than individual sessions, and they are an excellent way to give a child a taste of the game in a fun environment. Most youngsters enjoy the company of other children and they will often strike up friendships with like-minded young golfers. The one drawback, of course, is that children do not receive extensive personal attention, but any competent professional will keep the lesson flowing by holding frequent demonstrations that involve the whole group.

The process of finding a golf professional to teach a junior player should not merely be a case of phoning the nearest club and booking a series of lessons with the first available person. Parents should take the time to find out what each potential tutor has to offer; that way they can ensure that their child's first experience of a golf lesson is both interesting and enjoyable.

Ideally, parents should ask around for personal recommendations. Many coaches specialize in teaching different categories of player, so parents should seek out a coach with a good local reputation for working with juniors. Parents must also not be afraid to conduct a mini-interview, as any good golf pro will be perfectly happy to meet up and discuss their ideas. At this 'interview' stage, parents should assess the professional's personality and communication skills. The child should also attend this meeting, and parents should look to see whether the pro attempts to establish a rapport with the youngster. A good pro will address the child by their first name, he will also direct questions towards the potential pupil and, just as importantly, he will listen carefully to the answers the child gives. In most cases, a parent's instinct will quickly determine whether a professional is suitable or not. However, parents should also ask the child for their opinion, after all it is they who must attend the lessons.

CHOOSING A PRO

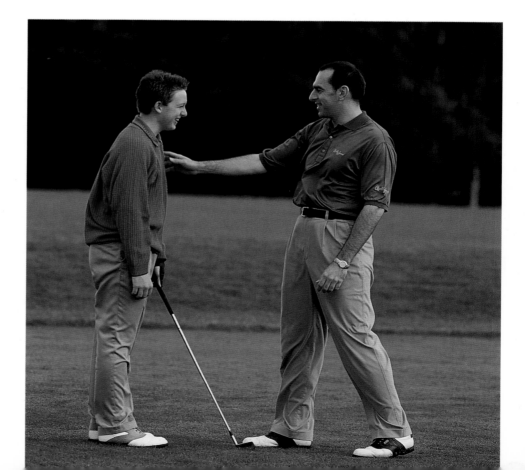

MAKE THE GAME FUN

Life is one big adventure for children and, to them, playing golf is no different. The best way of maintaining a child's interest level is to make the game fun. Parents, no matter how well-meaning, should never force the game upon their children. Ideally, youngsters should be introduced to the game gradually. Parents should start by letting their children watch them chipping and putting in the garden. Youngsters will soon want to join in with this garden golf, so mums and dads need to have a junior club handy for their golfing proteges.

Even once the child has developed a rudimentary swing and grip, practice sessions should remain relaxed through the use of achievable targets and light-hearted competition. Most children will not have the attention span to spend hours on the range fine-tuning their swing until they are in their early teens. Prior to this, youngsters need to experiment with playing a variety of different shots and should not focus on specific areas of the game for extended periods. Only once a junior has made it clear that he has the motivation to improve, should he be allowed to work on specific areas of technique.

ENCOURAGE PARTICIPATION IN OTHER SPORTS

Contrary to popular opinion, many of the world's top players were not particularly keen golfers as children. Lee Westwood's first sporting dream was to become a professional footballer, Nick Faldo was a very good cyclist before he got a taste for golf at the age of 14, while South Africa's Ernie Els was keen on rugby, cricket and was, by all accounts, an excellent tennis player, too. It wasn't until Els reached his mid-teens that he began to focus his attention on the game of golf. Even Tiger Woods, who apparently spent his infancy with a golf club in his hands, also enjoyed athletics and baseball.

Playing a selection of sports is an excellent way for a child to develop both fitness and co-ordination, so parents should not feel that they will hinder their child's golfing progress by encouraging them to play other sports.

ALWAYS BE A SUPPORTIVE PARENT

Golf is a very frustrating sport for the novice, so parents must be especially supportive of their children as they learn the game. In golf, the margins for error are tiny and it can take considerable time for a beginner to acquire the skills merely to make contact with the ball, let alone strike it with any control or authority.

Parents should try to empathize with their children, offering as much encouragement as possible during the difficult early phases of learning the game. Mums and dads must also try to avoid becoming frustrated when their child's progress is not as rapid as expected. Unfortunately, there are no short cuts to playing good golf. As long as children adhere to the basic fundamentals and continue to enjoy practising and playing, they will improve.

If a junior player has aspirations to become a professional golfer, parents must quickly inform themselves of the various options available to their child; in that way they can help him reach a sensible decision and develop a career path. The biggest decision the player must make is whether to try to become a club pro, who normally works at a golf club or driving range, or a Tour pro, who plays competitive golf for a living. Whichever path the youngster decides to aim for, parents should encourage him to hone his skills by playing in as many junior club competitions as possible.

The more competitive golf a youngster has under his belt, the better prepared he will be for the future. Head to head competition will not only sharpen young players' concentration, but also their ability to play under pressure. Similarly, Medal play, where every stroke counts, provides a great test of a junior's overall game.

In addition to the competitions organized by local clubs, there are also several Junior Tours that young players can compete on. These tours give youngsters a taste of what top-level competitive golf is all about. However, this fast-track approach is not suitable for all junior players, and it is important for parents to let their child develop at his own pace. No matter how talented a child is at golf, it's important that he have a well-balanced life with plenty of other interests. Pushy parents are rarely successful.

It's natural for parents to want their child to win golf tournaments, even at a very young age, but it is important that they praise their child whatever the outcome. Reprimanding a child for not playing well, will put the youngster under pressure the next time he plays, and could also put him off the game for good. Parents should make time to give their child a reassuring hug when they come off the 18th green, regardless of whether the child has played well or poorly.

THE ASPIRING PROFESSIONAL

TOUR PRO OR CLUB PRO?

Many young golfers are attracted by the glamorous lifestyle of the game's top stars and develop aspirations to become Tour professionals. However, the competition for places on any of the pro circuits, let alone the main Tour, is fierce and the standard of play is extremely high and improving every year. For most youngsters, the best option is to join a golf club or driving range as an assistant professional and train for a diploma from the Professional Golfers Association (PGA). A young player's golf may suffer in the short term while they combine studying, working in the pro-shop and learning their trade, but if they don't make it onto a Tour, they will at least have the PGA qualification to fall back on. The PGA diploma enables the player to work at golf clubs and driving ranges throughout the UK and Europe.

THE CLUB PROFESSIONAL

Once a player has a handicap of four or less, he can register to become a member of the Professional Golfers Association (PGA). Many golfers start as an apprentice to a senior professional while they are still teenagers, spending four years learning their trade under the senior pro's supervision. The PGA's training covers a variety of topics, including retailing and merchandising, club repairs, swing theory, accounts and teaching skills.

Many juniors, however, are under the misconception that as professional golfers they will spend every working hour playing golf. Unfortunately, this is rarely the case. Most good professionals will try to give their assistants time to get out on the course and maintain their skills, but if a youngster is working in the shop and studying hard, such time will be at a premium.

At the end of their training period, newly qualified professionals receive a diploma. The new pro must also decide whether to stay on as an assistant professional at his current club, whether to apply for a Club Professional post elsewhere or, if he has the ability, to try to qualify for a Tour Card. There are also several less obvious career paths open to the PGA Qualified professional. Nowadays, it's not just golf clubs and driving ranges that employ golf professionals – hotels, golf stores and golf schools all actively look to employ good quality professionals. A PGA qualification is highly respected.

THE TOUR PROFESSIONAL

Golf has become such a competitive sport that it is now extremely difficult for players to make it on Tour without first having several years of full-time playing experience. Although there are amateurs who have turned pro and qualified for the main Tour at the first attempt, such examples are rare. Most professionals work their way up through the ranks via various mini Tours and smaller feeder Tours, gaining vital experience along the way. By the time most players feel ready to enter the PGA European Tour Qualifying School they have plenty of competitive golf under their belts. And even then, there are no guarantees that they will make it.

It takes a certain type of person to succeed as a Tour Professional and it's not always the most talented players. Just because a young player has won everything in sight as an amateur and is shooting course records in every competition, doesn't necessarily mean he will have the temperament to make it on Tour. At the very top level of golf, mental strength is equally as important as technical ability. After all, any player good enough to have obtained a Tour Card is obviously highly skilled. At the pinnacle of the game, it is attitude more than aptitude that separates winners from journeymen.

Sweden's Per-Ulrik Johansson, for example, never won anything of significance as an amateur, but he won the Belgacom Open in his Rookie Year on Tour in 1991 and has gone on to enjoy a very successful career, twice representing Europe in the Ryder Cup. At the other end of the scale, England's Michael Welsh won just about every amateur honour as a schoolboy, yet, thus far, he has failed to make any significant impact on the professional Tours.

In general, successful Tour Pros are extremely confident and self-centred. This may sound a little harsh, but it takes a certain degree of arrogance to be able to stand on the first tee in a tournament and believe that you are going to win. However, that's precisely the level of self-belief that a young player needs if he is to stand any chance of realizing his ambitions.

Then there's the lifestyle. Players say that it takes at least a full season to get used to the travelling. Jetting around the world every week sounds like a great way to make a living, but the novelty of departure lounges, cramped aeroplane seats and living out of a suitcase soon wears off – particularly if you're flying back home on Friday afternoons, not Sunday evenings, having missed the cut.

This may be a rather pessimistic view of life as a Tour Pro, but it is important that young players understand the whole picture. Of course, if a player makes it big, the inconveniences become somewhat insignificant. With millions in the bank and a private jet, the top Tour pro can enjoy an enviable lifestyle. The competition is, however, extremely intense.

FIRST LESSONS — THE IMPORTANCE OF GOOD BASICS

3

If a player does not have a sound grasp of the basics, his golf swing will be a disaster waiting to happen. A golfer who aims the clubface carelessly or who has a poor grip and a sloppy posture will have to compensate for these flaws later on in his swing. And the more compensations that a player makes, the more chance there is that things will go wrong.

Tour Professionals spend more time fine-tuning and tinkering with the intricacies of their set-up than any other area of their game. The top players know that if they encounter a problem with their swing out on the course, 99 times out of 100 it can be traced back to a fault at address. Junior players should follow the lead of Messrs Faldo, Norman and Els by keeping a regular eye on the basics of their game.

FIRST THINGS FIRST, LEAVE IT TO THE PROS

Before any adult attempts to shape a child's swing, it's imperative that the youngster has a sound understanding of the fundamentals of the game. Under the supervision of a PGA qualified professional, juniors should learn how to hold the club correctly, stand to the ball, aim the clubface and adopt a good posture. Parents should not be tempted to teach their children these vital components of the golf swing. Bad habits groomed at a young age are very hard to break several years later. Children should be given the best possible start by learning the fundamentals from a trained professional.

The renowned golf teacher John Jacobs once said that he had yet to encounter a 'good golfer who played with a bad grip'. While Jacobs' view is somewhat extreme, the point he was making – that the grip is the foundation of a good swing – is valid. The grip is the only contact a player has with the golf club, and so great care must be taken over it.

A neutral grip, where neither left nor right hand dominates, gives the player the best possible chance of returning the clubface squarely to the target line at the point of impact. The grip will also determine a player's wrist hinge, the plane of his swing and the amount of power he can generate.

A GOOD GRIP

PARENTAL TIP

AVOID RECOMMENDING A STRONG GRIP

Some coaches recommend that children start by holding the club with a slightly 'stronger' grip. It is argued that this grip, if employed while youngsters are still growing in strength and size, will help the young player release the club. However, in most cases this approach should not be followed. Bad habits, and especially those concerning the fundamentals of the swing, are difficult to shake off later, so it's best to make holding the club correctly an instinctive part of the game.

FOUR STEPS TO THE CORRECT GRIP

Top players are very careful about the way that they form their grip, and junior golfers must be no less disciplined. A good grip should be as natural as possible. If a players stands up and lets his arms hang naturally by his sides, his palms and forearms turn inwards slightly towards his thighs. This should illustrate to golfers how their hands should look when holding the golf club. Players should follow this procedure to ensure that they are holding the club correctly. When the hands are moulded together like this, the player has the best chance of hitting a powerful accurate shot. The guidelines on the following pages are written for a right-handed player; swap left for right and vice versa if the player is left handed.

 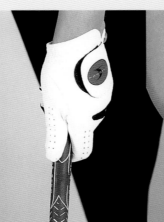 

1 Players should allow the grip to run along the base of the fingers on the left hand. The index finger is used to form a slight 'trigger'.

2 As the player closes his hands around the club, he should be able to see between two and three knuckles on his left hand. The left thumb should be just to the right of centre on the grip and pointing straight down at the ground.

3 As the player positions his right hand on the club, the grip should rest in the fingers of his left hand.

4 The grip is completed when the player closes his right hand so that the lifeline on the right palm rests on top of the left thumb, covering it completely. If the grip is made correctly, the player should be able to see two knuckles on his right hand.

QUICK TIP

GRIP CLUB IN FINGERS FOR EXTRA POWER

A common mistake among golfers of all ages and abilities is to grip the club too much in the palm of the hands – a fault which is often difficult to spot since the grip can still look perfectly good from the outside. Although it may feel more solid and powerful when the player holds the club in the palms of his hands, it can actually cost him distance because the wrists cannot hinge correctly. Think about how you would skim a pebble across a pond. You instinctively hold the stone in your fingers and then 'snap' it across the water with your wrists. You would not hold the stone in the palm, and the same concept applies to golf. So if a player's shots lack 'life', the answer is likely to lie with the grip.

NEUTRAL GRIP
With a neutral grip a player should be able to see the same number of knuckles on each hand.

STRONG GRIP
If a player can see more than three knuckles on his left hand and fewer than two on his right, the grip is too strong.

WEAK GRIP
If a player can see fewer than two knuckles on his left hand and more than two on his right, the grip is too weak.

EQUIPMENT TIP

CHECK YOUR GRIP SIZE
A player whose clubs are fitted with grips that are either too small or too big for his hands, will find it difficult to form the correct grip. If the grips are too large, he may find it difficult to get his hands around the club, which will prevent him from hinging his wrists correctly during the backswing and releasing the club through impact. The net effect of all this is likely to be sliced shots.
If, however, the grip feels too thin in a player's hands it's likely that his hands will be overactive, which can often lead to hooked or pulled shots to the left. With a correctly sized grip, the tips of the fingers should just touch the pad of the hand when the player holds the club.

YOUR GRIP OPTIONS

There are several ways that a player can link his hands together on the club. Tiger Woods and Jack Nicklaus favour the interlocking grip, but most other top players use the overlapping (or Vardon) grip, while many coaches recommend that juniors start off using the baseball grip. The decision is really one of personal choice, so youngsters should be encouraged to try out all the main types of grip before settling on the method that they find most comfortable.

THE BASEBALL GRIP

Juniors are often encouraged to use the baseball grip. Because the hands are placed side by side on the grip, without any link, there's more freedom of movement, making it easier to hinge the wrists and release the club.

THE VARDON GRIP

Named after the famous English golfer Harry Vardon, this grip is often referred to as the overlap grip, as the little finger on the right hand rests in the groove between the index and second finger on the left hand. This is the most popular grip among low-handicappers.

THE INTER-LOCKING GRIP

The interlocking grip, which is the preferred grip of Tiger Woods, is favoured by golfers with small hands. It is similar to the Vardon grip, but the little finger on the right hand and the left index finger interlock rather than overlap.

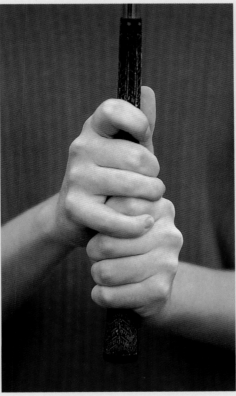

THE ADDRESS POSITION

The way in which a player stands to the ball is called his 'address position', and the quality of this position has a marked influence on the outcome of any shot. Most poor swings are caused by flaws at address, so players must strive to ensure that their stance, alignment and posture are correct.

POSTURE – PRIMING THE SWING

There are two reasons why good posture is essential for playing good golf. The first is that if a player is well-balanced at address, it's easier for him to transfer his weight back and through correctly and, therefore, it will be easier for him to strike the ball powerfully. Secondly, the angles created with the body determine the shape and plane of the swing and, as a result, its efficiency and power.

The key to a successful address position is to make it as natural as possible. Players should not bend excessively from the hips, nor should they flex their knees so much that their backside almost touches the ground.

To attain the correct posture, the player must grip the club then raise it in front of himself until the shaft is parallel to the ground. From here, he must bend forward from the hips, keeping his lower back straight. If this procedure is followed correctly, the player's backside should stick out a little as he lowers the club to the ground. Finally, he should flex his knees just enough to add a little spring to the legs, though not so much that height is lost.

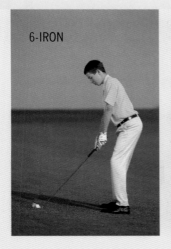

6-IRON

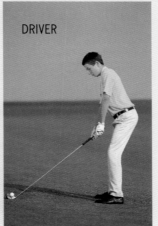

DRIVER

CHANGING POSTURES FOR DIFFERENT CLUBS

If you look at these two pictures, you'll notice that the player's posture changes according to the club used. Because the driver has a longer shaft and a flatter lie, players need to stand a little more upright than when hitting mid-irons, which are shorter in length and also more upright. The shortest and most upright clubs of all are the short irons and wedges, which require players to create more of an angle with the upper body in order to get lower down to the ball.

QUICK TIP

HOW MUCH KNEE FLEX?

Most golfers are aware that they have to flex their knees as they address the ball, but many players (old and young) get confused about how much they need to flex their knees. One point worth remembering is that too much knee flex is equally destructive to the swing as too little. The knees only need to be lightly flexed, and the best way to discover the right amount is to stand facing a full-length mirror. The player should be able to flex his knees a little without affecting his height. This level of flex is ideal.

STANCE AND BALL POSITION

The width of the stance and the ball position should vary according to whichever club the player is using. For a driver, where clubhead speed is normally the aim, a wide, solid swing base is called for, whereas with the middle and short irons, the emphasis is very much on accuracy, so there is no need for the stance to be as wide.

DRIVER

Ideally, a player's shoulders should fit just inside the width of his stance. If the stance is narrower, the player risks losing his balance during the swing. However, a stance that is excessively wide will prevent the hips and shoulders from turning fully.

In addition, because of the lack of loft on the clubface, players should look to strike the ball slightly on the upswing to get it airborne. The ball should, therefore, be played well forward in the stance, opposite the left instep.

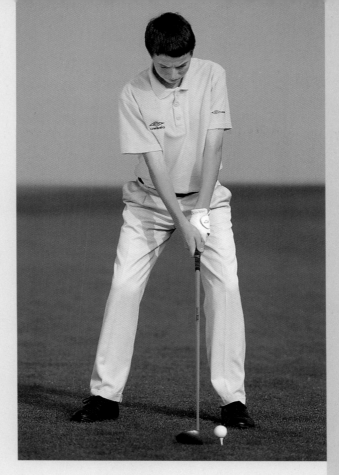

IRONS

With the shorter irons and wedges, the stance doesn't need to be as wide as when hitting a driver. The feet should be about shoulders-width apart for a mid-iron, and slightly narrower for wedges. These short irons are designed to be struck with a slight descending blow, so, as the clubs decrease in length, the ball should be played progressively further back in the stance towards the middle of the player's feet.

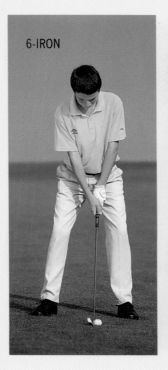

6-IRON

PITCHING WEDGE

TWO WAYS TO LOOK AT BALL POSITION

There are two schools of opinion regarding ball position. The first argues that the ball should be played one inch (2.5cm) or so inside the left heel with the driver, moving back in the stance as the clubs shorten in length until, with the wedges, it is played approximately in the centre of the feet.

The second theory is that the ball position should remain consistent, opposite the leading armpit, regardless of the club length. Many coaches believe that this approach leads to a consitent swing, as the width of the stance becomes the only variable factor in the set-up.

Each theory has its merits and its high-profile supporters. Young players should, as always, be encouraged to experiment until they decide which method they favour.

Most amateur golfers pay very little attention to their alignment; however, every top professional is obsessive about it. Most amateurs struggle to hit the ball straight, but the world's top golfers find the target with laser-like accuracy. You don't have to be a genius to work out that, unless a player can aim the clubface and the body correctly, he has little chance of striking the ball accurately, regardless of how good his swing is.

The main thing for young players to remember is that, although they should always aim the clubface at the target, their feet, hips and shoulders must all aim parallel to and left of this line (right if left handed). If this sounds a little confusing, you may find it useful to visualize a railway track. The ball, clubface and target are the outer rail, while the feet and shoulders are the inner rail.

GOOD ALIGNMENT

QUICK TIP

GET A FRIEND TO CHECK ALIGNMENT

It is not easy for a player to check his own alignment while standing over the ball. Laying a club on the floor, parallel to the target line, will help players to set up squarely to the target when practising on their own. However, a more reliable method is for players to get a friend to check their aim. A second pair of eyes is invaluable, as even the smallest of flaws at address can cause big problems with the swing.

If you watch the world's top golfers in action, you will notice that, without exception, each has a routine that is unerringly followed before each shot. Whether hitting a driver off the first tee or a simple approach shot with a pitching wedge, the top stars never alter their routine.

There are several reasons why the top players are so precise about their pre-shot routines. Firstly, they know that the quality of their shots is largely determined by the quality of their basics (i.e. the way in which they grip the club and address the ball). By incorporating these fundamentals into a routine, the player maximizes his chances of settling into the correct address position.

Secondly, human beings are creatures of habit. We perform tasks more effectively after repeated rehearsal. If a routine is ingrained enough, it will automatically be followed as soon as the club is taken out of the bag. And, if the first part of the routine is the same every time, the last part – in this case the golf swing itself – will also be the same.

Take Nick Faldo, for example. If you time his routine from the moment he picks up his club until he starts his backswing, you will find that it varies by no more than a fraction of a second for each shot he plays. In addition, if Faldo is disturbed while going through his routine, he

PRE-SHOT ROUTINE

1

2

will start again from the beginning, even going so far as putting the club back in the bag and taking it out again.

A player's pre-shot routine is unique to him and is full of idiosyncrasies. There are, however, several components that young players should be encouraged to incorporate into their routines. Firstly, once the player has assessed the shot and is comfortable with his club selection and strategy, he should stand directly behind the ball to target line and visualize the shot he is about to play (1). The next move for a right-handed player is to approach the ball from the left, stepping into the shot with the right foot setting the clubface behind the ball, while the right hand aligns it square to the intended line of flight (2). The player should complete his stance by bringing his left foot forward, ensuring as he does so that his feet aim parallel to, but left of, the target (3). Once he has applied his left hand to the grip, he should check his aim, giving the club a quick waggle to relieve the tension in the forearms. Only should he then set his swing in motion (4).

Always practise efficiently. Get into the habit of laying a club or umbrella on the ground square to your target line so that you can consistently monitor your alignment. Use this time to groom your pre-shot routine as well as your swing.

3

4

THE LONG GAME

According to an old golfing cliché, 'you drive for show and you putt for dough'. However, like most clichés, this saying is based on an oversimplification. Putting is undoubtedly a very important part of the game, but so too is the long game. After all, you can only putt for birdies and pars if your long game is good enough to get you to the green in the first place.

If a player can hit long, straight drives he will leave himself shorter approach shots into the green, which in turn will lead to shorter putts for birdies and pars and, finally, better scores. There's no doubt that length off the tee – as long as you are accurate too – is a huge advantage because it normally means that you can use a more lofted club to play your next shot. If you need further proof of just how important the long game is, just look at a selection of the world's best players. Tiger Woods, David Duval, Ernie Els, Davis Love III and Colin Montgomerie are all known more for their driving prowess than their short game and putting.

So with that exciting thought in mind, let's take a look at the golf swing and the long game in a little more detail.

THE GOLF SWING

One of the best ways to learn about the golf swing is to study the techniques of the world's top players. Sweden's Per-Ulrik Johansson has one of the most efficient swings in the world of professional golf. Most young players could learn much from his method.

SWING SUMMARY—CHEST ON VIEW →

1 With an iron, the player's hands should be slightly ahead of the ball (as demonstrated by Per-Ulrik) with his weight evenly balanced and feet about shoulder-width apart.

2 The clubhead stays low to the ground for the first few feet of the swing. At this point, the player's shoulders begin to turn in response to the swinging motion created by his arms.

1 At address, Per-Ulrik adopts an athletic posture, with his body aligned squarely to the target. The body angles created here will be maintained throughout the whole swing.

2 At the top of the swing, his hands are above the right shoulder, with the clubshaft square to the target line. See how the spine angle remains as it was at address and how the knees are still flexed.

3 At impact, Per-Ulrik's hips are open to the target, while his shoulders are in virtually a square position

4 Even in the follow-through position, you can still see the angles Per-Ulrik created at address.

3 By the time he reaches the top of the backswing, his wrists should have fully hinged and his shoulders should have turned 90°. See how both of Per-Ulrik's knees remain flexed and how the right knee in particular has resisted the turning of the upper body.

4 A good downswing starts from the ground upwards. From the top of the swing, the player nudges his left knee towards the target and begins to clear his hips out of the way. He should also retain his wrist angle for as long as possible into the downswing.

5 The moment of truth. At impact, the shaft of the club and left arm should form as straight a line as possible in order to apply maximum pressure to the ball. Most of the player's weight should now be on his left side.

6 A good follow-through is the product of a good swing. Weight should be on the player's front foot, and his chest should be facing the target. All the spikes on the player's back foot should now be visible.

THE THREE KEYS TO A SOLID SWING

Because of its speed and complexity, a golf swing can be difficult to break down into its constituent parts. However, it is only by dissecting the swing that faults can be isolated and remedied. For the purposes of this book, we have broken the swing down into three key elements.

PRACTICE EXERCISE

THE BEST EXERCISE FOR YOUR GAME — THE PIVOT DRILL

This exercise should be practised as often as possible, as it is the best way to develop the correct body movement. The player should set up normally and then, holding a club behind his back, turn his shoulders so that the shaft of the club points in front of him. As the player turns his shoulders, he must retain the angle of his spine and resist the turn with his right knee, which should remain constantly flexed. If this exercise is performed correctly, the player should feel slight tension in his right thigh. In the downswing, he must rotate his body into the follow-through position, once again making sure that he maintains his spine angle and the flex in his knees.

SWING KEY 1. MAINTAIN ADDRESS ANGLES THROUGHOUT THE SWING

The key to consistent ball-striking is to retain the flex in the knees and the angle of the spine (which is created when the player tilts forwards at address) throughout the whole of the swing. If the legs straighten or the spine angle changes during the swing, the club will be thrown off plane. The result will be unpredictable and unimpressive.

In this particular swing sequence you can see how the player keeps the angle of his spine in the same position throughout – even into his follow-through.

SWING KEY 2. AS ARMS SWING, WRISTS HINGE

As the player swings the club away from the ball – while retaining the flex in her right knee – the weight of the clubhead should automatically force her wrists to hinge and the clubshaft to point toward the sky. This motion is called the 'wrist set' and it stores up power for later in the swing.

If a player's wrists do not hinge correctly it's likely that she is holding the club too tightly. If he relaxes his grip pressure a little, he will feel the weight of the clubhead more easily and his wrists will be more responsive. Relaxed wrists are vital for good ball-striking, so encourage players to let them hinge a full 90° if necessary. If a player's grip is correct, she will easily control the hinge of her wrists.

SWING KEY 3. FOR MAXIMUM POWER, DON'T FORGET TO RELEASE THE CLUB

Assuming that your pupil retains a correct body angle and a smooth wrist hinge in the backswing, the only thing left to worry about is 'releasing' the club through impact. If you have ever played tennis and hit a top-spin winner down the line, you will already have a good idea of what the release should feel like.

In the downswing, the player must focus on allowing his right forearm to roll over his left. This motion will impart 'draw spin' on the ball, which will cause it to fly almost straight, with just a slight curve from right to left.

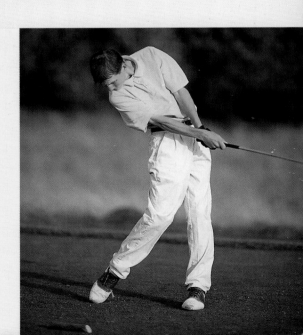

THE DRIVER SET-UP

The priority for shots played with the driver is to create clubhead speed, and to maximize this your pupil will need to start from a solid base. Set him up with his feet just over shoulder-width apart.

Remember, the aim should be to sweep the ball off the tee peg and into the air with a shallow angle of attack. To make this easier, the player's weight should favour his right side at address and the ball should be played well forward in the stance, just inside the left heel. His hands should be level with, or fractionally behind, the ball at address.

1 The swing should start smoothly, with the clubhead low to the ground to set up a wide takeaway. This is the longest club in the bag, so encourage youngsters to give themselves plenty of room.

THE DRIVER SWING

DRIVING — SWEEP THE BALL AWAY

The driver, which is usually used to hit tee shots on par-4s and par-5s, is the club that hits the ball furthest. However, it is also the longest and least forgiving club in the bag, which is why it's vital the set-up and swing are as accurate as possible. Players may get away with small flaws in their swing when playing with shorter irons, but with the driver, any faults are ruthlessly exposed.

2 The shaft should reach a position where it is parallel to the ground at the top of the backswing. It's very important that players control this power. To do this they must retain the flex in the right knee and prevent weight from moving onto the outside of the right foot.

3 To maximize power, the player must make the transition between backswing and downswing as smooth as possible. Any sudden lunges will destroy rhythm and almost certainly lead to a loss of power and distance.

4 At impact, the left arm and club should form a straight line as the clubface makes contact with the ball slightly on the upswing as the clubhead is released past the body.

5 The finish position. The player's weight should now be supported by his left leg and right toe and his chest should be facing the target.

QUICK TIPS

THE CORRECT TEE HEIGHT
The purpose of the driver is to sweep the ball away off the top of the tee peg. A small but important point for all players to consider, is the height to tee the ball. Ideally, you should be able to see the top half of the ball above the top of the clubhead at the address position.

AIM AT TINY TARGETS FOR BETTER ACCURACY
If a younster's driving accuracy leaves something to be desired, try this simple tip, which many Tour Pros use. Instead of aiming just anywhere down the fairway, ask the player to pick out a really small target in the distance. It can be a branch on a tree, a chimney on a house, anything that he can focus on. By aiming at a tiny target, he will narrow his margin for error and give his brain a clear instruction. The wider your target, the wider the scope for inaccuracy.

COURSE MANAGEMENT

Being able to plot your way around a golf course from the first hole to the 18th green, safely avoiding the pitfalls of bunkers, rough, lakes and ditches, requires patience, strategy and intelligence. Collectively, this is called good course management and it's something every top player excels at. Good golf is smart golf and to become really good players, juniors must learn a wide range of course management skills.

WORK YOUR WAY BACK FROM GREEN TO TEE

When standing on the tee, players should have a strategy or game plan for every hole. First, it must be decided which side of the fairway offers the best angle of attack into the green. For example, if there are bunkers protecting the front right side of the green, it will obviously be safer to hit an approach shot from the left side of the fairway where it won't be necessary to carry the ball over the sand.

Having decided which side of the fairway to aim at, players must next ensure that there are no hazards, like fairway bunkers or lakes, waiting to catch them out. If the chosen route does encounter hazards, players can either select a club which won't reach the hazards, or play well away from the trouble. Alternatively, if the hazards are too great, players may want to re-think their shot strategy. The best players are those who have a game plan, but who aren't afraid to change it if necessary.

TAKE FULL ADVANTAGE OF THE TEEING GROUND

In golf, every detail counts. Depending on the shape of the hole, most top players will tee up on the side of the teeing ground that gives them the safest route to the fairway.

Colin Montgomerie, for example, likes to fade the ball – curve it slightly from left to right in the air – so he will usually set up on the right side of the teeing ground and aim down the left edge of the fairway. This way he has the full fairway to aim at.

ON LONG PAR-5S, LAY UP TO YOUR FAVOURITE DISTANCE

A good habit for any youngster to copy is laying up on par-5s. If the green is well out of reach, this tactic can be a very positive move. Rather than trying to blast the ball as far up the fairway as possible and bringing all kinds of hazards into play, most top players will deliberately try to leave themselves a full shot of around 100 yards (91m) into the green. So if the green is out of reach, encourage youngsters to play a shot that will then enable them to play an approach shot into the green with their favourite club.

PLAY TO 'SAFE' PARTS OF THE GREEN

If you watch golf tournaments on television, you will have noticed that the pros don't always aim at the flag when they're hitting their approach shots into the greens. The reason for this is because the green-keepers like to place the pins in really difficult positions on the green – for example, just behind a bunker or right next to the water. These are called 'sucker pins' because only a sucker would aim at them.

In such situations, the professionals normally aim at the safe part of the green because they know that if they aim at the flag and mis-hit their shot, they will probably end up in the sand or the water. This is not negative play it's smart play.

MAKE THE WORST SCORE A BOGEY

When many junior golfers run into trouble on the golf course, they make things worse by trying to play a miraculous recovery shot.

Colin Montgomerie's attitude to a poorly played shot is to make sure that his worst score on the hole is a bogey. For example, if Monty hits his tee shot into the trees on a par-4 (which he doesn't do very often) and has no safe route to the green, he will play a shot that enables him to go for the green with his third shot – even if it means chipping out sideways back onto the fairway.

This does not mean that you should encourage youngsters to settle for making a bogey every time they hit a wayward shot. On the contrary. Much of the fun in golf comes from using the imagination to conjure up adventurous recovery shots. However, youngsters should be taught to carefully weigh up their chances of pulling the shot off. If in doubt, take the safe option and make the worst score a bogey.

When you find your ball nestled in the trees, it is normally best to chip back onto the fairway.

QUICK TIPS

KNOW YOUR YARDAGES

Even young players should know how far they can hit the ball with each club, as this will enable them to hit their approach shots confidently. If they don't have this information, their club selection will be little more than guesswork. Players should hit ten golf balls with each club, ignore the best two and the worst two shots, then take an average of the remaining six balls. This will give an accurate guide to the distances they can achieve with each club.

ALLOW FOR A 'FLYER' OUT OF LONG GRASS

Many players do not expect to be able to hit the ball very far out of long grass, but occasionally the exact opposite happens and the ball flies further than from a clean lie on the fairway. This is known as a 'flyer' and it happens when blades of grass get trapped between the ball and the clubface at impact. This situation prevents the grooves from imparting backspin on the ball. As a result, the ball flies further than normal.

THE SHORT GAME — TECHNIQUE, TOUCH AND IMAGINATION

5

Hitting booming drives and powerful iron shots may look impressive, but no matter how consistent a player is from tee to green, he will always find himself chipping and putting to make par several times during every round. Even the best players only hit 13 to 14 greens in 'regulation' per round. This means that superstars like Tiger Woods and Lee Westwood regularly rely on their short game to keep their scores ticking over.

It is no good getting up to the green in two shots if it then takes three to get the ball in the hole. According to the pros, the best players are those who can put a good score together even when they're not swinging well. Players who chip and putt well can afford to miss a green, safe in the knowledge that they have another two chances – a chip and a putt – to save their score. Another benefit of a good short game is that it gives confidence to the rest of a player's game. If a player believes he can chip and putt to save par should he miss a green, he will be less inhibited in his approach play.

The good news is that almost anyone can improve their short game. It takes neither fantastic athleticism nor timing to hit a chip shot or stroke a putt. All a player needs is a basic understanding of the technique and the desire to improve.

QUICK TIP

START WITH CHIPPING AND PUTTING

One of the main reasons that Sergio Garcia, Jose Maria Olazabal and Tiger Woods are so deadly around the greens is that they learnt to chip and putt before they progressed to making full swings. Spain's Seve Ballesteros is another player who spent countless hours around the green conjuring up all kinds of different shots, and the skills he developed in those early days have lasted his whole career.

Chipping and putting requires no great physical strength, so parents should encourage their children to develop these aspects of their game. In fact, many of the world's top coaches recommend that children start by mastering putting before moving further away from the hole as their strength and skills develop.

THE 3-STEP SHORT GAME PLAN

STEP 1. DEVELOP THE BASICS FIRST

It's often said that good touch and imagination is the key to a sharp short game. However, a player will only be able to visualize a shot and accurately judge pace and distance once he has a solid technique that he can rely upon. If a player is unsure whether he will catch the ball too thin, a little heavy or just right, he will neither be able to picture the shot in his mind nor judge its power. To avoid this problem, junior golfers must first develop reliable chipping, pitching and bunker play techniques. Only once a reliable action has been groomed should the youngster begin to attempt some of the more 'adventurous' recovery shots.

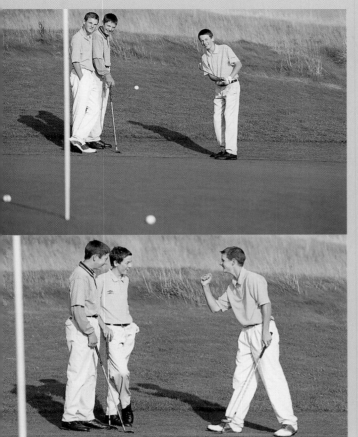

STEP 2. WORK ON TOUCH AND FEEL

Once a player has developed a consistent technique, he will find that his touch and feel for distance improve very quickly. When you see the top players hitting shots around the practice area during a tournament, most of them are simply keeping their eye in, rather than working on their technique. Although it's definitely a good idea for players to review their action regularly, once the basics are mastered, practice time should be devoted to developing 'feel'.

One of the best ways for a player to quickly improve his skills around the green is to practise with a friend. A little friendly competition re-creates the pressure of an on-course situation and improves concentration. It's also more fun to practise with a friend, rather than hit ball after ball on your own.

STEP 3. DEVELOP AN OVERACTIVE IMAGINATION

Many children are told that they have an over-active imagination, but when it comes to the short game, vivid imagery is no bad thing. In fact, it's a real bonus. Most player have to work hard to improve their visualization skills. Before a player decides on what type of shot he wants to play, he must first be able to 'see' it clearly in his mind. Visualizing a shot is simple for a straightforward chip shot from the fringe but, unfortunately, players will only rarely find their ball lying cleanly on a flat piece of turf with no obstacles blocking the route to the hole. The more difficult the situation the player finds himself in, the more innovative and confident he must be. Creative flair and the ability to manufacture a shot in seemingly impossible circumstances set the masters of the short game apart from those who are merely competent around the green.

Short game magicians such as Seve Ballesteros, Jose Maria Olazabal and Sergio Garcia have all hit countless practice shots to develop their skills around the green, and there are no short cuts. Young players who want to succeed must spend hours around the green, rehearsing techniques, experimenting with different clubs and making mental notes of how the ball flies and rolls from a variety of lies and slopes.

CHIPPING

A chip shot is played from around the edge of the green and is intended to loft the ball over the longer 'fringe' grass or rough and onto the putting surface. Once on the green, the chip shot should roll the rest of the way along the ground just like a putt. The aim is to put the ball close enough to the hole to leave a very short putt. In fact, many top professionals are such expert chippers that they are often disappointed if they don't hole the shot.

One of the reasons that the top pros are so confident is that they treat the chip shot as an extension of their putting stroke. Many players even use their putting grip to play the shot. The idea is to get the ball running on the green as soon as possible, so a neat and compact stroke with very little hand action is best employed. Only rarely will a top professional loft the ball high into the air from around the green. The best players know that it is easier to judge the shot and control the ball when it's rolling along the ground.

Some players have a favourite club that they use to play the majority of their shots around the green, but most will use anything from a 4-iron to a sand wedge, depending on how far they are from the hole and how much rough they need to clear first. Young players should practise their chipping with three clubs – a 5-iron, an 8-iron and a sand wedge – so that they are able to deal with a range of distances. In addition, juniors should strive to learn how the ball reacts off the clubface of any given club, and they must also learn to judge the speed of the shot.

BASIC CHIPPING PRINCIPLES

The basic chip is one of golf's most simple shots. The swing is short – back and through – and it does not require any great hand-eye co-ordination. However, despite its simplicity, many golfers make a mess of this shot. There are two main reasons why players fluff a chip shot. The first is that they try to add extra loft to the clubface by scooping the ball into the air. This approach will see the player either catch the middle of the ball with the leading edge, sending it racing across the green at 100 mph, or stub the clubhead into the ground behind the ball. If you watch the world's top players, you'll see that their hands lead the clubface through impact. This guarantees a crisp strike and ensures that the ball stays low to the ground.

The second likely cause of a failed chip shot is a lack of acceleration through impact. Many golfers make a good backswing then completely quit on the shot. With a fairly short swing, players must keep the clubhead accelerating smoothly through the ball. Loss of speed leads to loss of control.

THE BASIC CHIP SHOT

1 The chipping set-up should be geared towards control and accuracy. The player shuffles his feet fairly close together and, keeping the ball just behind centre in a slightly open stance, eases his weight onto his front foot so that he leans toward the target. Following this routine will set the hands ahead of the clubface and the ball.

2 Keeping his weight on his left side, the player swings the club away with his arms and shoulders. It's perfectly acceptable for the wrists to hinge a little in response to the weight of the club, but players shouldn't try to hinge them on purpose. The backswing should be compact.

3 Assuming that a player has kept his weight on his left side throughout the swing, his hands should automatically return to their address position and lead the clubface through impact. The player should feel as though he is hitting down on the ball with a descending blow. This action is the key to imparting a little check spin on the ball.

4 The player stays down through the shot and waits until he has struck the ball before looking up to see where it has gone. He should make sure his hands remain ahead of the clubface well into his follow-through.

CHIP SHOT CHECKLIST
- Take a narrow stance
- Play the ball back of centre in stance
- Lean into the shot with weight on front foot
- Set hands ahead of clubface at address
- Allow arms and shoulders to control swing
- Choke down on the grip for control
- Keep hands ahead of the ball through impact

Short game practice is more enjoyable if there's a little friendly rivalry or competition involved.

CHIPPING PRACTICE AND STRATEGY

EXPERIMENT WITH DIFFERENT CLUBS

No two chip shots are the same, so the ability to judge distance and select the correct club is vital. Players should practise chipping with a selection of clubs so that they get used to the carry and roll of each iron. Using the same length swing, a shot played with a 5-iron, for example, will carry further and roll more on landing than one with a pitching wedge, which will hit the ball higher into the air and stop it quicker.

CLUB	CARRY	ROLL
SAND WEDGE	90 PER CENT	10 PER CENT
PITCHING WEDGE	80 PER CENT	20 PER CENT
9-IRON	70 PER CENT	30 PER CENT
8-IRON	60 PER CENT	40 PER CENT
7-IRON	50 PER CENT	50 PER CENT
6-IRON	40 PER CENT	60 PER CENT
5-IRON	30 PER CENT	70 PER CENT
4-IRON	20 PER CENT	80 PER CENT
3-IRON	10 PER CENT	90 PER CENT

ALWAYS TRY TO LAND THE BALL FIRST BOUNCE ON THE GREEN

When playing a chip shot, a golfer's aim should be to get the ball on the green and rolling towards the hole as soon as possible. Unless there is no other option, players should avoid trying to run the ball through rough or long fringe grass, as it is impossible to know how the ball will react. It could get a nice bounce and run onto the green without any problems, but it could just as easily get snagged and caught up in the longer grass, leaving the player facing yet another chip shot. To be on the safe side, players should try to carry the ball a yard or so onto the green.

Chip shots, which stay low to the ground, are preferable in many situations, but there are times when such 'safe' shots are not an option. For example, when the pin is cut close to the front edge and there is a lot of rough to carry, a high, 'floaty' shot may offer the only chance of getting the ball close.

The first thing a player must do when playing a lofted shot is to check the lie. If the ground is dry or bare, he should forget it, as the leading edge of the clubface will bounce off the ground and into the back of the ball. The result will be a thinned shot that races across the green. Players should only attempt to play this shot if they can get the clubface under the ball.

The lob shot may sound complicated and daunting, but once the mental barrier of having to make an almost full swing for a short-range shot is overcome, confidence quickly grows. The good news is that it's a fun shot to work on. By varying the stance and angle of clubface, players can produce shots of different trajectories.

THE LOB SHOT

1

The technique for a lob shot is similar to a bunker shot (see pages 84–91). An out-to-in swing path is required, as this cuts across the ball to give it extra height. Players need to set up with shoulders fairly square to the target but feet aiming left – the more the player opens his feet, the higher the ball will go. The player's weight should favour the left foot, and the ball should be played forward in the stance. He aims the clubface at the flag, then grips the club.

2

The player swings back along the line of his feet, hinging his wrists early in the backswing to pre-set a steep angle of attack. Remember that it is the loft on the clubface combined with the open stance that creates height, so players must make a long backswing just to carry the ball a short distance. However, a longer swing involves extra risk, so a smooth tempo is required for this shot.

3

The downswing should follow along the line of the feet. The player will probably find it strange to swing across the target, but as long as he aims the clubface correctly at address, the ball will fly towards the flag. He must, however, make sure that he does not release the club, otherwise the ball will fly to the left.

4

Because this shot is normally played from a fluffy lie a player must create a fair amount of clubhead speed through impact. Whatever distance he swings back, he must follow-through by about the same amount. The backswing and follow-through must mirror each other.

DOWNHILL CHIP

1 When a player sets his shoulders level to the ground on a downslope like this, his weight will automatically fall onto his front foot. This is not a problem, but he will need to widen his stance a fraction to give himself extra stability. He will also need to play the ball a little further forward to compensate for the fact that his weight is on his left side. In addition, he may want to choke down on the grip by about one inch (2.5cm) or so to give himself more control over the shot.

2 To avoid swinging straight back into the slope, the player will probably have to hinge his wrists a little earlier than normal. Keeping his weight on his left side, he should swing the club away with his arms. To the player, this action will feel as though he is picking the club up steeply in the backswing with his wrists.

When playing from any kind of sloping lie, either on the fairway or around the green, the player should set up with his shoulders as close to parallel to the ground as possible. That way he effectively recreates a flat lie, which will enable him to play the shot using only a slightly adapted version of his normal swing. Another secret is knowing how the slope will affect the flight of the ball. The downhill chip is very tricky as the ball shoots off the clubface low and fast.

3 The clubhead should stay as low to the ground as possible in the downswing. The player should feel as though he reaches down for the ball with his arms extended. The clubhead should 'trace' the contours of the slope and slide under the ball.

4 To guard against trying to scoop the ball into the air, the player should keep the clubhead low to the ground well into the follow-through. Try to keep the arms extended for as long as possible to ensure that the clubhead slides underneath the ball and follows the contours of the ground.

PITCHING

A pitch shot is one step up from the chip shot and for an amateur its range is from 30 to 70 yards (27–64m) of the green. The pitch is played with a longer swing and a more lofted club – usually a pitching wedge or sand wedge. The aim of this shot is to send the ball into the green fairly high, so that it stops quickly and rolls only a short distance once it lands.

Pitching is one area of the game where the pros put amateurs to shame. Tour Professionals will look to hit the ball to within ten feet (3m) of the flag from shots of 100 yards (90m) or less, but most amateur golfers are satisfied merely with getting the ball onto the green.

The main reason for this lack of confidence is that, because the pitch requires a less than full swing, it is easy for players to lose their timing. As a result, the swing feels awkward and unnatural. Timing and tempo are the keys to consistent pitching. There's no magical secret to mastering this shot. The pitch simply requires an abbreviation of the normal, full swing with a few minor adjustments to the set-up to help reduce the distance the ball travels.

Players can improve their mental attitude toward pitching by viewing it as an attacking option, rather than as merely a recovery shot. Young players should be made aware that good pitching will not only help them save pars, but also help them pick up birdies on par-5s and short par-4s. However, before players can land the ball on a sixpence from 50 yards (45m), they must first develop a solid technique.

THE BASIC PITCH SHOT →

Many amateurs mistakenly believe that there is a magical secret to the pitch shot, but it's merely a shortened version of the full swing. However, retaining a smooth rhythm and tempo are just as important as the minor amendments players must make to their set-up.

A CHIP OR A PITCH?

Describing the difference between a chip and a pitch can be confusing because the two shots often overlap. Many golfers think a chip is played from short range, while a pitch is played from further out. There is a certain amount of truth in this view, but it does not tell the whole story. For example, you can play a bump-and-run chip shot from 50 yards (45m) from the flag on a fast-running seaside links course, or a pitch from 30 yards (27m) into a soft, receptive green.

A chip is a shot where the hands do not pass hip height (top) and it is played with very little wrist hinge. Once the hands progress past hip height and the wrists begin to hinge, the chip becomes a pitch (bottom).

1 The player takes a slightly narrower stance than normal, with the ball in the centre of his feet. Players should ideally also set up slightly open, with their feet aiming a fraction left of the target line. This gives more room to swing the arms through impact without the left side getting in the way.

2 From the amended address position, the player makes his normal swing. He must focus on maintaining a fluent rhythm as he swings his arms away. As with the full swing, the arms should remain tucked into the side of the chest and not move away from the body and the wrists should hinge gently, but fully.

3 With this shot, the emphasis is on accuracy rather than power, so there's no need for any excessive lower body action. The player controls the shot by rotating his upper body back and through. The ball is simply left to get in the way of the swing.

4 As with the chip shot, the player must avoid trying to scoop the ball up into the air. He must, instead, trust the loft on the clubface to get the ball airborne. As with the lob shot, the length of the follow-through should mirror the length of the backswing.

QUICK TIP

JUDGING DISTANCE
THREE CLUBS, THREE SWINGS, NINE DISTANCES

Mastering the pitching technique is a step in the right direction, but even then the job is not complete. It is also important for players to be able to judge how far they will hit the ball with each club. Through painstaking practice, the world's top players develop a fantastic sense for distance, but junior players must initially find a way of accelerating the learning process.

One good way of improving distance control is to use three clubs for pitching – 9-iron, pitching wedge and sand wedge. Starting with the sand wedge, the player makes a note of how far he can carry the ball when swinging back to hip, chest and shoulder height. This gives him three different distances. He can then do the same with the pitching wedge and 9-iron, making a written or mental note of the results. At the end of this process, he will have nine different distances at his disposal.

BUNKER PLAY — MUCH EASIER THAN IT LOOKS

6

Bunker play is a unique area of the game, with its own principles and techniques. Firstly, in the sand wedge golfers have a club that, though specially designed to help play out of the sand, never actually makes contact with the ball. Secondly, several important amendments must be made to the normal address position to play the shot correctly. And lastly, bunker play will induce more headaches than any other aspect of the game.

One of the most impressive sights in golf is that of a top player making a long, lazy swing and popping the ball out of a bunker. When weighing up an approach shot into the green, a top pro will not be too worried about finding the sand. Given the choice of playing out of a perfectly manicured bunker or from long, tangly fringe grass, where it may be difficult to predict exactly how the ball will come out, the pro will opt for the consistency of the sand virtually every time.

Technique aside, the number one key to bunker play is confidence. If a player steps into the sand in a positive frame of mind he will have every chance of successfully completing the shot. However, if he stands over the ball with negative thoughts buzzing around inside head, he has little chance of making the authoritative swing which is required to propel the ball out of the sand.

↓ THE SAND WEDGE — DESIGNED TO HELP YOU OUT

One of the main reasons that top professionals are so confident about playing from the sand is that they understand how to take advantage of the design of the sand wedge in order to make the shot easier. So, advise your pupil to invest in a sand wedge at the earliest opportunity.

Take a close look at the base of a sand wedge and you will notice that, unlike the rest of the irons, it has a wide sole. You will also see that the back of the club is set slightly lower than the leading edge of the clubface. This feature is called the 'bounce' and enables the wide part of the sole, rather than the thin leading edge, to make contact with the sand. The clubhead is, therefore, literally able to bounce through the sand taking a thin, shallow divot. The bounce angle becomes even more noticeable if the clubface is opened up. A skilful golfer will vary the angle of the clubface to create shots of different heights and trajectories.

BASIC BUNKER PRINCIPLES

↑ SWING ACROSS THE TARGET LINE

One confusing aspect of bunker play is that players are told to open their stance at address but to swing across the target line from out to in. The reason for this is that the address position takes its lead from the design of the sand wedge. When the clubface is opened to make full use of the 'bounce' on the sole, the club aims to the right so to compensate the player must aim left. All young golfers must understand the need to swing along the line of their feet and shoulders, no matter how strange it feels. Remember, the club aims right, the player aims left and the ball flies straight.

THE GOLDEN RULE – NO BALL/CLUB CONTACT

The sand wedge is a unique club not only because it is designed for a specific purpose, but also because it should never actually touch the ball. You may have heard TV commentators refer to a greenside bunker shot as a 'splash' or 'explosion' shot. The reason for this is that the objective is not to strike the ball with the clubface, but to propel it out of the bunker on a thin cushion of sand. In effect, the player creates a mini explosion by hitting approximately 1 inch (2.54cm) behind the ball. The theory is simple: if the golfer can remove the sand from the bunker, he will remove the ball, too.

1 The player shuffles his feet into the sand to lower the base of his swing and to get a solid stance. The clubface is opened before gripping the club. The stance is open too, with the weight slightly on the front foot. The ball is forward in the stance, the clubhead hovers over the intended point of entry in the sand — 1–2 inches (2.5–5cm) behind the ball.

2 The player swings back naturally along the line of his feet and hinges his wrists earlier than normal. This type of swing will encourage the splashing action as the clubhead enters the sand. Even on a short-range shot, players must use a relatively long backswing to overcome the resistance of the sand.

THE SPLASH SHOT SWING

HOW MUCH IS ENOUGH SAND?

If you asked three professional golfers to tell you how much sand they take with a bunker shot, you would probably end up with three comletely different answers. New Zealand golfer Frank Nobilo likes to take 1½ inches (3.75cm) of sand before the ball, as he believes that this approach offers the best combination of spin and release. However, Nobilo also says that, as long as you make contact with the sand 1–2 inches (2.5–5cm) behind the ball, you'll get the same result.

If a player takes 1 inch (2.5cm) of sand, the ball will travel further but will stop quickly on landing because of the spin, while if he takes 2 inches (5cm) of sand, the ball won't travel as far, but will release and roll more once it hits the green.

3 Keeping his eyes focused on the intended entry point in the sand, the player swings back down along the line of his feet and accelerates the clubhead down into the sand. Encourage youngsters to give the sand a good 'thump'. It requires considerable clubhead speed to remove the sand and the ball from the bunker.

4 If a player manages to keep the clubface in an open position throughout the swing, and accelerates smoothly and positively through impact, it should be possible to make it through into a full finish. The grooves on the clubface should point to the sky after the follow-through.

RULES AND ETIQUETTE

THE CLUBHEAD MUST NOT TOUCH THE SAND AT ADDRESS
A bunker is deemed to be a hazard and, therefore, players are not allowed to ground their clubhead at address. If the clubface touches the sand prior to a swing, the player will incur a two-shot penalty. Also, unless there is a local rule to the contrary, players are not permitted to remove stones or other loose impediments.

ENTER AND EXIT THE BUNKER AT ITS LOWEST POINT
To avoid damaging the bunker and displacing too much sand, remind youngsters to enter and exit the bunker at its lowest point, even if it means they have to take a longer route.

UNPLUGGING A BURIED LIE →

Although this shot looks nasty, it is not as difficult as it appears. All the player needs to do, is reverse every principle that applies to the normal splash shot. Whereas a normal bunker shot is one of controlled delicacy, unplugging a buried lie requires a more forceful approach. Top players will occasionally adopt a more subtle approach, but for youngsters the aim is simply to get the ball out of the bunker and safely onto the green at the first attempt.

ADVANCED BUNKER SHOTS

Straightforward bunker play can be difficult enough, but there are also times when the ball doesn't find a nice, clean lie in the sand. Unfair as it may seem, dealing with such shots is as much a part of the game as playing from perfect lies, so young players must learn to cope with these situations too. One thing they will quickly realize is that awkward lies arise more frequently than perfect ones.

THE UPHILL SHOT AGAINST THE LIP →

When a ball runs into a bunker at a fast pace, very often it ends up on a slight upsweep against the lip (see pic 1). The lie looks intimidating, but its not as bad as it seems. Firstly, the upslope acts as a launch pad for the shot, which means that getting the ball out first time should not be too difficult. Secondly, because of the extra height generated by the shot, a positive swing can be used, safe in the knowledge that the ball won't run too far.

1 With a splash shot, the clubhead skims through the sand, but with this shot it is the leading edge that digs into the sand. The clubface is closed and the ball is played back towards the middle of the feet. To create the steep downward attack into the ball, the player sets most of his weight on his left side.

2 To pre-set a steep attack into the ball, the player should place his weight on his left side, hinging his wrists immediately in the backswing. He must feel as though he is lifting the club straight up, swinging back to at least shoulder height.

3 With his weight on his left side, the player accelerates the clubhead down into the sand, making sure that the leading edge of the clubface makes contact with the sand first. Depending on how deeply the ball is buried, the resistance of the sand will prevent a full follow-through. The ball will come out low, fast and with little spin. Consequently, it will roll a long way once it hits the green, so plan the shot carefully.

1 At address, shoulders should be set level with the slope. This will cause the player's weight to fall onto his back foot. The clubface must remain square or slightly open to the target.

2 To generate enough forward momentum on the shot, a fairly long backswing is needed. The player's weight must remain on his back foot throughout the backswing.

3 Take about 1 inch (2.5cm) of sand before the ball and encourage your pupil to give the ball a good hard thump at impact. The upslope and the resistance of the sand will stop him hitting it too far.

4 The upslope of the bunker will restrict follow-through, so don't expect to see a full finish position.

PUTTING — THE GAME WITHIN A GAME

7

Professionals spend more time practising their putting than any other area of their game. This is because around 40 to 50 per cent of the strokes taken during 18 holes are putts. Before and after a tournament round, you will find the pros on the practice green working on their technique. Putting practice may not be as enjoyable as hitting balls on a driving range or pitching at a target, but the results are certainly worth the effort. The player who picks up the winner's cheque at a professional tournament will invariably average no more than 26 or 27 putts per round. By contrast, most amateurs struggle to take fewer than 40 putts per round.

However, there's no physical reason why junior players can't improve their putting statistics. Of course, the greens that youngsters play on at weekends and school holidays aren't as true as the manicured surfaces that the top players take for granted, but there's nothing stopping a dedicated junior from getting his putting average down to the low thirties at least.

As with the rest of the short game, a player doesn't need to be an amazing athlete to become a good putter. The putting stroke itself is relatively simple, so success depends mainly on a player's ability to read greens. The art of putting is essentially about judging speed and line, and once a player has mastered these skills, his handicap will spiral downwards.

PUTTING BASICS

THE PREFERRED PUTTING GRIP — THE REVERSE OVERLAP

Most top players use a different grip for putting than for hitting full shots. This is because, with the full swing, the wrists need to hinge, but in the putting stroke they don't. When putting, all the hands do is hold the club.

A variety of different grips are used by professional golfers, but the most common is the reverse overlap, which is similar to the normal overlapping grip (see page 46), except for the left index finger, which extends downwards, overlapping the first three fingers on the right hand. Placing the hands together like this enables them to work more as a unit, which makes it difficult for the wrists to hinge and, thereby, reduces the player's control over the stroke.

THE PUTTING SET-UP

The hole is only 4¼ inches (10.8cm) wide, so a player's alignment is even more important when putting than it is for a normal shot where the aim is a fairway or green many yards wide. The priority is to ensure that the putter face aims at the intended line, which (as is explained below) isn't always the most direct route to the hole.

Once a player has correctly aimed the putter face, his next goal should be to make himself comfortable. The arms should hang naturally from the shoulders, with eyes as close as possible to directly over the ball. Many coaches believe it's vital to have the eyes right over the ball for the best possible view of the line, but it's not essential, as by this time the player has already aimed the putter.

There are no hard and fast rules concerning the putting address position, but it's a good idea for a player to have his feet a comfortable distance apart. The player should also play the ball forward in his stance (towards the lead foot). As with the driver, the intention when using the putter is to catch the ball slightly on the upswing so that top spin helps it hold its line and reach the hole.

THE PUTTING STROKE – GO WRISTS-FREE FOR SAFETY

The first thing young players must remember when putting is that the usual wrist action which helps get the ball in the air on full shots isn't necessary during the putting stroke. It is worth noting that very few of the game's top players have a wristy putting stroke. This is because, with such a stroke, it is difficult to develop a consistent action.

Most professionals use what is known as a pendulum-style stroke, whereby they rock their shoulders up and down to create an even-paced stroke. The thinking behind this approach is that the larger muscles in the shoulders are more reliable than the smaller ones in the arms and hands. The pendulum method gives consistent results when employed by players who have a good touch and feel. However, for players who struggle with distance control, this approach should not be recommended, as it takes the hands and arms completely out of play. Beginners will find it easier to control the stroke with a combination of arms and shoulders.

THE PUTTING STROKE

1 At address, the player keeps his hands level with the ball and settles his weight evenly on both feet. He grips the putter lightly for maximum feel and, to enhance the pendulum movement, keeps his arms gently extended.

2 The player moves the putter away smoothly, with arms and shoulders working together. He keeps the putter head as low to the ground as possible. On short putts the putter should move away from the ball on a straight path, but on longer putts the putter head will naturally move inside the line.

3 It is important to maintain a consistent tempo throughout the swing. While player watches the putter head make contact with the ball the back of his left hand moves through toward the target. The stroke is a positive one, and the putter moves consistently forward through impact.

4 The putter face continues to aim at the intended line well into the follow-through. The player should stay down until the ball has left the clubface and is on its way to the hole. Players should not be tempted to have an early peek to see if they've holed the putt or not.

LONG PUTT STRATEGY — PACE IS MORE IMPORTANT THAN LINE

Most disappointing three-putts are caused, not by poor accuracy, but by leaving the ball well short of the hole with the first approach putt. Even relative novices will rarely miss a four-foot (1.2m) putt, but all too often players leave the ball further from the hole after their first putt. Therefore, it should be remembered that, when it comes to long putts, pace is more important than line. If the weight of a putt is good, players can afford to misjudge the line by a few feet and still leave an easy tap-in for their next shot.

PUTTING STRATEGY

Most golfers give very little thought to putting. More often than not, a player will take only a quick look at the hole before making his stroke. At the other end of the scale, the top professionals are very careful about the way in which they analyse their putts. They know that mistakes on the greens can be very costly, so they give all their putts maximum concentration.

QUICK TIP

AIM THE LOGO AT THE LINE
An excellent way for a player to aim his putter face correctly, is to mark his ball, then turn it so that the manufacturer's logo points directly toward the intended line. Now all he must do is set the putter face square to the logo and complete the stance. One the player is lined up, he can go ahead and make a smooth confident stroke.

SHORT PUTT STRATEGY —
TAKE THE BREAK OUT OF PLAY

On long-range putts, the priority is to judge distance correctly, but on short putts it is line that is most critical. All too often, missed putts from between three and four feet (0.9-1.2m) are caused by a lack of confidence. Players often make the mistake of trying to 'trickle' in shots that need to be played with a positive putting stroke. Two of the world's best putters, Tiger Woods and Colin Montgomerie, knock in the short putts with a firm stroke. This method means that all the player need worry about is the initial line, because after that, he knows that the ball won't have time to break.

GREEN-READING ROUTINE →

In order to develop long-term consistency in green-reading skills, it is important to encourage junior golfers to run through a specific routine as they prepare for a putt. Only by viewing each putt from the same angle, and by making the same number of practice strokes each time, will players be able to obtain consistent feedback on their judgement. Here are a few ideas to help youngsters improve their green-reading skills. At the same time, it's important to remind junior golfers not to study putts for too long as this can hold up the pace of play.

READING GREENS

All juniors must learn the basic skills required to accurately judge the pace and line of a putt. This process, which is often termed 'reading a green', is one of golf's great challenges. Players are unlikely to face exactly the same putt twice, and they are also unlikely to find a totally flat green, so the ability to read a green accurately is vital. In most cases, players will need to aim either to the right or left of the hole in order to allow for the 'break'.

Deciding on the line and speed of a putt is something the top pros excel at, but it is a skill which develops only with the experience of playing on a variety of courses in a variety of conditions. However, regular practice will accelerate the learning process.

1 Putts should be viewed firstly from behind the ball and then from behind the hole. This approach gives players the best chance of predicting the way in which the ball will move across the putting surface. By looking from behind the hole, in addition to the standard view from behind the ball, players gain a different perspective of the undulations of the green.

2 For long putts, players should walk to a point halfway between the ball and the hole on its lowest side. This position is particularly useful as distance is best gauged from a central point, while the severity of the slope is best judged from a low vantage point.

3 Players should remember to follow their pre-shot routine, making a practice strokes while looking at the hole to enhance their hand-eye co-ordination. Let your eyes compute the distance.

4 The putter should be aimed at the intended target line (not necessarily at the hole). The feet and body should then be aligned square to that line.

QUICK TIP

START TO READ THE GREEN AS YOU WALK ONTO IT

Players cannot afford to wait until they are standing on a green to start reading a putt. It is often difficult to detect the contours of the putting surface when standing on it, so players should, instead, start to read greens as soon as they are within pitching range. In many cases, players will get a better overall picture from slightly further away, where they can see the entire green and the lie of the surrounding land.

TREAT EVERY PUTT AS A STRAIGHT PUTT

← Reading a green is one thing, finishing the job is another. Once a player has picked out the line of a putt, he should aim the putter at his intended line and then align his feet and shoulders squarely to that point. In the case illustrated here, the ball will break by about two feet (60cm) from the right, so to compensate the player aims his whole body right of the hole. To help to focus on a chosen line, players can pick out an intermediate target along their intended line. They can then concentrate on simply rolling the ball over their chosen spot. In this sense, every putt is a 'straight putt', regardless of how much break there is, because once a player has selected his intermediate target, he no longer needs to consider the contours of the green.

FACTORS THAT AFFECT BREAK

Observation is the key to reading greens, and any clues that reveal how the ball will break are invaluable. After a while, players begin to take in all kinds of subtle information, like the texture of the green, the length of the grass and even the weather, to help judge break.

When teaching a junior how to read a green, it is important to make them aware of the following factors, each of which can affect the pace and break of the ball:

1. SPEED OF THE GREEN

The ball will break more on fast, dry greens than on slow, wet ones. Players should also take into account the strength and direction of the wind when assessing the putt, particularly if the green is very exposed.

2. GRADIENT

The ball will break less on an uphill putt than on a downhill one. This is because players have to hit the ball more firmly on an uphill putt to get it to the hole, consequently, the speed of the ball prevents it from breaking too much.

QUICK TIP

CHECK ROUND
THE HOLE FOR CLUES
If you watch a top player reading a putt, you'll notice that they nearly always have a good look at the area of green around the hole. They know that as the ball reaches the hole it will be running out of steam and, therefore, will break more during the last few feet of the putt than at any other time. Inspecting the slope around the hole helps players decide how much break to allow for when lining up a putt.

LESSONS AND PRACTICE

No matter how much talent a player has, he will never get by on natural ability alone. Ask any Tour Pro to reveal the secrets of his success and he will most likely tell you that it's down to regular lessons, plenty of practice and the desire to succeed. The world's top golfers constantly strive for perfection and the stunning golf that you see at televised tournaments is the product of painstaking hard work that is carried out behind the scenes and away from the cameras.

It's no coincidence that the game's most successful players have been the hardest workers. When he was regarded as the world's No.1 in the early 1990s, Nick Faldo would think nothing of hitting 1,000 golf balls a day, and that was before he began work on his short game and putting. Similarly, Jack Nicklaus would be out on the range beating balls come wind, rain or shine and the legendary Ben Hogan, by his own admission, literally dug the secret to the golf swing out of the dirt with hundreds of thousands of divots.

Many amateurs wonder why players like Ernie Els and Tiger Woods still need a coach when they are clearly such accomplished golfers. However, the truth is that it always helps to have a second set of eyes, if only to give the player extra confidence about the state of his game. Even the top stars suffer from recurring swing faults, but such problems can quickly be identified and cured by a coach who has enough background knowledge of a player's game.

So if regular lessons and practice are essential for the superstars of the game, you can imagine just how important they are for a player who is just starting out. In this chapter, we'll look at how young players can get the most out of their lessons, how they can structure practice sessions and how they can select a coach who will help them realize their potential.

THE IMPORTANCE OF LESSONS

When considering taking golf lessons, players should be aware that there is no point in booking just one. Golf is a very complex sport and it cannot be mastered overnight. Developing a solid and consistent swing takes time and, therefore, a long-term view has to be taken.

Junior players should also understand that merely attending lessons is not enough to transform them into a good player. In between sessions, players need to knuckle down and practice so that they can consolidate what they have been 'taught'. A player who goes home after a session and forgets about his golf until the next lesson, will find himself going over the same ground week after week.

FINDING THE RIGHT COACH

As is explained earlier in this book (see page 42), there's more to arranging golf lessons than picking up the phone and dialling the first number advertised. Ideally, players should try to find a coach with whom they can develop a working relationship. Before committing to a series of lessons, juniors should meet up with the pro and discuss their game. Most golf professionals will happily set aside a few minutes to answer any queries or questions. The most important thing players should assess at this stage, is a professional's commitment level. The best pros are the ones who are enthusiastic about teaching and passing on their knowledge of the game to keen students.

WHAT YOUR PRO EXPECTS FROM YOU

The first thing a golf pro hopes for from a pupil is a willingness to learn. Golf lessons are expensive, so players must be prepared to throw themselves heart and soul into learning the skills of the game. If they do this, then most pros will do their utmost to help them. However, if a player is simply going through the motions during a lesson, the pro is likely to be similarly uninterested. Only inspired pupils receive inspirational teaching.

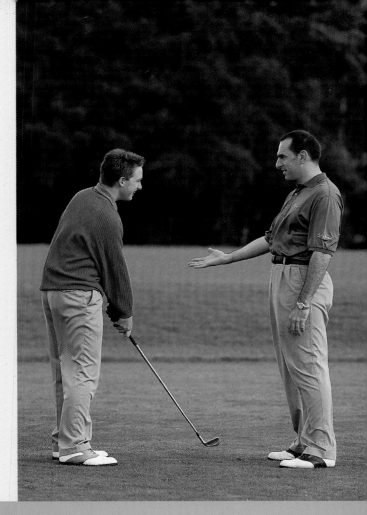

QUICK TIPS

ARRIVE EARLY TO LOOSEN UP BEFORE LESSON

Very often, the first five to ten minutes of a lesson are wasted while the student hits balls to loosen up. This is dead time that the pupil is paying for. To avoid this situation, the player should arrive at the golf club or the range 15 minutes early to hit a few balls and do some simple stretches. By doing this, he will be raring to go as soon as the lesson starts.

MAKE YOUR NORMAL SWING IN FRONT OF THE PRO

When a pupil is asked to hit some balls for a teaching professional, it is vital that the player uses his normal swing. All too often players put on a show that doesn't reveal the faults in their swing. Explain to juniors that booking a lesson with a pro and then being too self-conscious to display your normal swing is like making an appointment to see the doctor when you're ill, but pretending there's nothing wrong when you get there.

To help a player make the most of his ability, the pro must see his swing with all its quirks and flaws. If the pro only gets the censored version, the player will be wasting both time and money.

Many golf teachers now use a video camera during lessons. The video is used to film the pupil's swings from several angles for initial analysis. Some teachers still believe that their eyes are good enough to pinpoint faults in the swing, but a high-speed video camera which is capable of recording up to 8,000 frames per second leaves nothing to doubt.

Used correctly within a lesson, the video benefits both the pupil and the teacher. From the pupil's point of view, it's always interesting to see your swing on video because, more often than not, it looks nothing like you had imagined. For the teacher, the video will often highlight flaws that are only detectable by watching a slow-motion version of the swing

Another benefit of the video camera is that the pro and pupil can sit down together and talk through the swing, frame by frame if necessary, and discuss the key lesson points. It is, however, worth remembering that most players find the first viewing of their swing on video a disconcerting experience. Players will inevitably focus on the things they do wrong, but a good pro will also use the video to highlight the things the player does well, not just the weaker areas of his game.

USING VIDEO IN LESSONS

AVOIDING VIDEO OVERDOSE

Although the introduction of high-speed video has improved the quality of teaching over the past 15 years or so, one downside of this technology should be explained to every pupil, particularly juniors.

There is a thin dividing line between using video as a helpful and informative part of the teaching process and becoming totally dependent on it. The tell-tale sign of video overdose becomes apparent when a teacher seems more concerned with what a player's swing looks like than its effectiveness on the course.

Good teaching professionals will normally use the video for an overview of a player's swing and to help their initial analysis, but will thereafter use it only occasionally, perhaps to highlight a change or to emphasize a key point.

As it is very difficult for a player to watch his own golf swing, a second pair of eyes can be invaluable for spotting faults in technique.

Colin Montgomerie, Europe's best player in the late 1990s, says that if he caddied for an amateur golfer he would dramatically improve their score without making any kind of changes to their swing. That's some claim, but the point he is making is that one major difference between a top class professional and an amateur golfer comes in their course management, i.e. the way they plot their way around the golf course and avoid trouble by thinking smartly. Monty believes that if he told the player which club to hit, read the greens for them and advised them on their strategy, he would knock at least four shots off their normal score.

Of course, no junior player will be lucky enough to find Colin Montgomerie caddying for him, so instead, players should book a playing lesson with a teaching professional. This is usually a little more expensive than a normal half-hour session because of the extra time involved, but, for a junior player, it is a useful and informative way to spend a couple of hours.

Firstly, a playing lesson enables the pro to get an idea of how a player's overall game is developing – something that is impossible to gauge on a driving range. Secondly, it gives the pupil the opportunity to study the playing habits of a good golfer. In particular, juniors should closely observe the way the professional thinks his way around the golf course.

THE BENEFITS OF PLAYING LESSONS

QUICK TIP

ASK FOR A SHORT GAME LESSON

If a player has problems with his short game, it is well worth requesting a short game lesson. Many players are reluctant to seek advice on their chipping and putting, but lessons in these areas are just as important as those for the long game. The good news is that learning the basic chipping, pitching, bunker play and putting skills is usually a far quicker process than mastering the full swing. What's more, it'll be a refreshing change for the pro, too, who spends 99 per cent of his time giving lessons on the swing.

PERFECT PRACTICE

Contrary to popular opinion, it is not practice, but perfect practice, which makes perfect. A player who goes to the driving range and hits 200 balls as hard as he can with a driver, will do more harm to his game than good. Good exercise? Possibly. Good practice? Most definitely not. It's far better for a player to hit just 20 shots, each of which is given his full concentration, than to slam 100 shots away mindlessly without a second thought as to what he's doing.

When a junior player leaves the practice ground at the end of a lesson, he's left to fend for himself at the range and, without the reassuring presence of a pro to keep him on the straight and narrow, it's easy for him to slip into bad habits. All players must learn to structure their practice so that it is both constructive and progressive. The following routine will help young players to get the most out of every session at the range.

LEAVE THE PRACTICE SWING ON THE PRACTICE RANGE

One basic error that every golfer makes at some stage, is trying to work on their swing out on the course. Incorporating a new move into the swing is a positive step on the practice range, but on the golf course, players should get on with the business of playing the shots.

MAKE THE BALLS LAST LONGER

At the driving range it's very easy to tee up ball after ball in quick succession, only to find that your huge jumbo bucket of balls has disappeared after 20 minutes. Most players are better advised to buy a smaller amount of balls and make them last longer. Mandy Sutton, a professional on the women's European Tour, takes at least 45 minutes to hit 45 balls on the range. Sutton believes that this approach ensures she gives each shot maximum concentration.

STEP 1 – WORK ON TECHNIQUE

Firstly, players should get into the habit of setting up a 'practice station' at the start of each session. The station is created by laying down a couple of club shafts, which are used to monitor the player's alignment and ball position, thus ensuring that he hits every shot from the correct address position.

Secondly, although there may be several things that the player wants to work on in his swing, he should discipline himself to focus on just one thing at a time. He should begin without a ball, making a practice swing to concentrate on the specific feeling he is trying to achieve in the swing. Once this feeling is achieved, it should be repeated while hitting a shot. As soon as the feeling is lost, the player should go back to making swings without a ball until it is regained. He should hit between ten and 15 balls like this, before switching to Step 2 (right).

STEP 2 – FINE-TUNE THE ROUTINE

The next area of the game to focus on is the pre-shot routine. The slicker and more grooved this routine becomes, the easier it will be for the player to slip into auto-pilot out on the golf course. The pre-shot routine will also help the player achieve consistency.

The routine should be rehearsed as though the player was hitting each shot for real on the course. The player must stand behind the ball and visualize the shot, then set himself up correctly, developing a swing trigger. Gary Player liked to press his hands forward slightly before starting his backswing, while Jack Nicklaus swivels his head slightly to the right a split-second before starting his swing. The key is to keep each individual element of the routine in the same order each time. At this stage, the player shouldn't be too worried about his swing, as any concerns should have been dealt with in Step 1.

DON'T NEGLECT WEAKNESSES

It's human nature for players to practise things they're good at. Unfortunately, if a player neglects problem areas, he will struggle to improve his game in the long run.

Young players must be encouraged to identify the areas of the game that they find difficult. They must then try to dedicate practice time to working on these areas until they begin to enjoy playing the relevant shots. That's not to say that youngsters should not still play their favourite shots during practice, rather that their weaknesses must be given priority. Before long, the player will be hitting shots that previously they would have tried to avoid.

PLAY A ROUND
ON THE RANGE
In 1996 Nick Faldo won the
Masters, but going into the
tournament he wasn't playing
particularly well. Rather than
continue to hit poor shots,
which would have further
undermined his confidence,
Faldo struggled with his swing
on the range and changed his
practice routine. Instead of
working on his swing, he
decided to play the course on
the range. Starting with the
'first hole', he would hit a 'tee
shot', then according to where
he believed it would have
finished, he played the next
shot. This took his mind off his
swing and forced him to focus
on shot-making. The same
approach can be employed by
junior players to add variety to
sessions at the driving range.

OFF-COURSE PRACTICE

Practising your golfing technique at home can be a hazardous pastime. But don't worry, players don't have to aim through a tiny gap in the patio doors to improve their accuracy. In this section, we will look at ways that young players can work on their game away from the golf course, without destroying the family home at the same time.

CHIPPING PRACTICE WITH AN UMBRELLA

With a little imagination, an umbrella can be put to good use in dry weather to improve a player's short game. To practise their touch and feel for distance, players should place an opened umbrella on the ground upside down and simply chip balls into it from a variety of distances. This is a great way for golfers to learn what kind of loft can be expected from each club in the bag. Alternatively, the umbrella can be placed on the ground, approximately three inches (7½cm) behind the ball. This ensures the player avoids trying to scoop the ball into the air, and instead sets his or her weight on the left side and makes a steep up and down swing.

117

OFF-COURSE PRACTICE

OFF-COURSE PRACTICE

IMPROVE THE BASICS INDOORS

The most difficult changes to make to the swing are those relating to the basics of the grip, stance, alignment and posture. This is because any faults are usually so ingrained and feel so comfortable that golfers are reluctant to change.

A change to players' grip will, inevitably, feel awkward for a while, and they must expect to hit a few bad shots until the new method feels natural and comfortable. That's why it's a good idea for players to spend as much time as possible at home grooming the basics. For example, if a teaching professional recommends that a young player changes the way he or she holds the club, there's nothing to stop the player holding a golf club using the new grip while watching television during the evening. Similarly, players can easily check their posture and stance in front of a full-length mirror, and they can even monitor the plane of their swing in an uncluttered area of the house such as the hall.

CLIMB THE LADDER

Misjudging the speed on a long-range putt is usually the cause of a killer three-putt. Here's a good exercise to improve touch. Line up several balls at varying distances from the hole. Start from either near the hole or from the ball furthest away and try to hole each putt. This teaches you how to adjust your stroke to match putts of different lengths.

ROUND THE CLOCK

To practise your short range putting place sereral balls around the hole. Taking care to line each one up carefully, attempt to hole each putt. The beauty of this exercise is that you get to practise putts with a variety of different breaks, thereby preventing you from losing interest.

USE STATS TO HIGHLIGHT PROBLEMS

Many of the world's top golfers keep notes on their performances. Junior players should follow suit by recording and analysing the basic points of their game after every round. While playing, the youngster should make a note of how many fairways he hits, how many putts he takes, how many times he three-putts and how many times he got up and down to save par from off the green. This practice will highlight a player's strengths and weaknesses, making it easy to focus in on areas for improvement.

121

HONING A SQUARE-TO-SQUARE PUTTING STROKE

A good way for a player to test the quality of his putting stroke, is to lay down two club shafts on the carpet or lawn, parallel to each other and just over a putter-width apart so that they form a tram-line to the hole (upturned coffee cup). The player can now hit practice putts, ensuring that the putter head stays within the two shafts, moving fluently back and through. The results of this exercise are frequently impressive.

HEADS AGAINST THE
WALL FOR A SOLID STROKE

Moving the head during putting or looking up too early to see where the
ball has gone are two of the most common putting faults. These
problems are particularly destructive as they can throw the putter off
line and lead to all kinds of bad putts. A good way for a player to practise
keeping a steady head is to putt along the skirting board at home while
pressing their head lightly against the wall. This will encourage the player
to keep the head steady throughout the whole stroke.

123

SPECIAL GOLF QUIZ

This special quiz, which is organized in a four-round tournament format, has been designed for the junior golfer who wants to test his knowledge of the game against friends and family.

Each question has four different answers to choose from. All the player needs to do is select the right one. Just like golf, players will need skill, patience and, at times, a little bit of luck to post a really good score. And to give the uninitiated a chance, all of the answers can be found somewhere within the pages of this book.

Finally, and just like a golf tournament, if a player doesn't play well over the first two rounds, he'll miss the cut. So if you want to qualify for the final two days, you'd better start revising now. Good luck, good reading and good playing.

ROUND ONE – THE BASICS

1. Which is the most commonly used golf grip?
   a) The interlocking grip
   b) The baseball grip
   c) The Vardon (overlapping) grip
   d) The intermesh grip

2. How much should a player flex his knees at address?
   a) Not at all
   b) Just enough so that he doesn't lose any height
   c) So much that his bottom sticks out behind him
   d) So much that his thighs begin to feel tense

3. To hit a straight shot, where should a player's feet and body aim?
   a) Directly at the target
   b) Slightly right of the target
   c) Parallel left of the target
   d) Slightly left of the target

4. How wide should a player's stance be when hitting a driver?
   a) Just over shoulders-width apart for stability
   b) Very narrow to create extra power
   c) As wide as possible
   d) Feet together

5. What's the most likely outcome of a weak grip?
   a) A straight shot
   b) A hooked shot to the left
   c) A very high shot
   d) A sliced shot to the right

6. How can a player create the correct spine angle at address?
   a) By bending forwards from the hips
   b) By bending forwards from the waist
   c) By bending forwards from the rib cage
   d) By keeping the spine upright

7. How can a player get maximum wrist hinge and leverage?
   a) By gripping the club with the fingers
   b) By gripping the club in the palms
   c) By gripping the club tightly
   d) By using heavy golf clubs

8. Where in the stance should the ball be played for a wedge shot?
   a) Opposite the right foot
   b) Opposite the left heel
   c) Towards the middle of the stance
   d) Backward of centre in the stance

WRITE YOUR FIRST ROUND SCORE HERE:

YOUR FIRST ROUND SCORE
8/8 You're the clubhouse leader. Well done!
6–7 You're two-under par and in good shape.
4–5 Level par, but you're a little off the pace already.
0–3 A poor opening round of two-over par has put you in danger of missing the cut.

ROUND TWO — RULES AND ETIQUETTE

1. The Rules of Golf allow players to carry how many clubs in their bag?
   a) 12
   b) 14
   c) 10
   d) 20

2. If a player knows he's hit his ball out of bounds what should he do next?
   a) Replay his shot from the same place after adding one penalty stroke to his score
   b) Drop a ball, without penalty, next to where the original ball went out of play
   c) Drop a ball within two club lengths of where the original ball went out of play and add a penalty shot to his score
   d) Replay the shot without penalty

3. Where should a player leave his golf bag while putting?
   a) On the edge of the green itself
   b) Off the green, adjacent to the next tee
   c) At the front of the green
   d) On the fairway in front of the green

4. What should a player do as soon as he walks onto a green?
   a) Repair his pitchmark and mark his ball.
   b) Start to read his putt.
   c) Remove the flagstick from the hole
   d) Clean his spikes

5. What does it mean if a player has 'the honour'?
   a) He is best player in his group
   b) He is winning the match
   c) He has the right to tee off first
   d) He can choose which type of competition to play

6. What is a player not allowed to do in a bunker?
   a) Take his shoes off
   b) Use his putter to play the shot
   c) Let the clubhead touch the sand at address
   d) Shuffle his feet into the sand

7. How much time are players permitted to spend looking for a lost ball?
   a) 15 minutes
   b) 10 minutes
   c) 1 minute
   d) 5 minutes

8. What should a player always do at the end of the round?
   a) Shake hands with his playing partners
   b) Stand and mark his scorecard on the green
   c) Go straight to the practice range
   d) Count his clubs

WRITE YOUR SECOND ROUND SCORE HERE:

YOUR SCORE AFTER TWO ROUNDS
16/16   You're leading the tournament. Great play!
12–15   You're three-under par and still in contention
8–11   Level par, but you've got some catching up to do now
0–7   I'm afraid you shot four-over par and missed the cut. Better luck next time. Back to the practice ground

ROUND 3 — MISCELLANEOUS

1. It's sometimes possible to hit the ball further than normal out of long grass because:
   a) The grass creates extra height on the shot
   b) Grass gets trapped between the ball and the clubface, which prevents backspin
   c) Moisture from the grass prevents backspin
   d) The ball travels further when it hits the ground

2. To hit a driver well, the clubface needs to make contact with the ball:
   a) Right at the base point of the swing
   b) Slightly on the upswing
   c) Slightly on the downswing
   d) None of the above

3. What is the key to generating backspin?
   a) The quality of the strike
   b) The condition of the green
   c) Clean clubs and grooves
   d) All of the above

4. What should a player do when taking a shot from any kind of sloping lie?
   a) Set his shoulders square to the slope
   b) Change his swing plane
   c) Use a more lofted club
   d) Place more weight on his toes

5. What is the purpose of a pre-shot routine?
   a) To save time on the golf course.
   b) To achieve greater consistency
   c) To make sure the player doesn't lose anything
   d) To help hit the ball further

6. If the ball is above a player's feet, which way will it fly in the air?
   a) To the left
   b) To the right
   c) Very high
   d) Very low

7. Which Major Championship is played at the famous Augusta National golf course each year in April?
   a) The Open Championship
   b) The US Open
   c) The USPGA Championship
   d) The Masters

8. Why do many clubs request that players wear soft spikes?
   a) Because they are cheaper
   b) Because they do not damage the greens
   c) Because they grip better
   d) Because they are more comfortable

WRITE YOUR THIRD ROUND SCORE HERE:

YOUR SCORE AFTER THREE ROUNDS
24/24   You're still in the lead at six-under par and obviously in great form.
19–23   You're four-under par and in good shape to mount a last round charge.
13–18   You've slipped to one-over par and need a great last round .
8–12   You're struggling with your game and need a good last round to see your name on the leaderboard.

THE FINAL ROUND – SHORT GAME AND PUTTING

1. **The best place to view the distance and break of a long putt is:**
   a) Mid-way between the ball and the hole on the low side
   b) Mid-way between the ball and the hole on the high side
   c) From behind the ball
   d) From behind the hole

2. **To remove the ball from a buried lie in the sand, a player should:**
   a) Open his stance and the clubface.
   b) Close his stance and open the clubface
   c) Close his stance and the clubface
   d) Keep his stance and the clubface square

3. **When chipping, a player's strategy should be to:**
   a) Carry the ball as far as possible through the air
   b) Keep the ball on the ground as much as possible
   c) Use his favourite club all the time
   d) Use a lofted club all the time

4. **How much sand should a player take before the ball when playing a bunker splash shot?**
   a) 3–4 inches (7½–10cm)
   b) 5–6 inches (12½–15cm)
   c) 1–2 inches (2½–5cm)
   d) No sand at all

5. **Ideally, where should a player's eyes be looking when putting?**
   a) Directly over the line of the putt
   b) Inside the line of the putt
   c) Outside the line of the putt
   d) It doesn't really matter

6. **What does the term 'reading a green' mean?**
   a) Studying the details on the course planner
   b) Looking for the hole
   c) Judging the speed and the contours of the green
   d) Practising putting before playing the shot

7. **In which form of competition is a player allowed to 'give' his opponent a putt?**
   a) Medal play
   b) Match play
   c) Stableford
   d) Texas Scramble

8. **Which part of the sand wedge makes contact with the ball in a splash shot?**
   a) The leading edge
   b) The sole of the club
   c) The grooves
   d) No part of the club touches the ball

THE FINAL ROUND LEADERBOARD

32/32 Are you sure your name isn't Tiger?
Congratulations, you led the tournament from
start to finish like a true champion

25–31 Very well played.
You scored an excellent 6-under par and
if a few more putts had dropped you could have won it.

20–24 Well done.
You shot two-under par. You obviously have lots of
potential, but too many bogeys proved costly this time.

14–19 Not bad, but level par is only good enough to finish in
the middle of the pack. Head straight to the practice range.

8–13 You scraped into the last two rounds, but you'll need to
work a lot harder if you want to win.
Back to qualifying school, I'm afraid.

WRITE YOUR FINAL ROUND SCORE HERE:

GLOSSARY

An alphabetical explanation of some of the most common golfing terms

Address – Also known as the set-up, it is the starting point of the golf swing and incorporates the alignment of the body and the positioning of the feet and the ball

Albatross – A score of three under par on a hole.

Alignment – The direction in which your body aims at address.

Approach shot – A shot played into a green using a full swing.

Back-nine – The second set of nine holes on an 18-hole course.

Backspin – The rotation of the ball caused when it is struck by the clubface. Backspin helps get the ball in the air.

Baseball grip – Variation of the grip where the hands are not joined together.

Birdie – A score of one-under par on a hole.

Blade – A style of clubhead design usually use by good players

Bogey – A score of one-over-par on a hole.

Bounce – The angle on the sole of a sand wedge that prevents the clubhead from digging into the sand too deeply.

Break – The amount the ball will move in response to the slope on a green.

Bunker – A sand-filled hole, usually placed on the edges of the fairway and around the greens.

Carry – The distance from when a ball is struck to when it hits the ground.

Caddie – A person who carries a golfer's clubs around the course.

Cavity-back – A style of clubhead design where weight is taken from the centre of the club and redistributed around the edges to make it more forgiving.

Chip – A shot played from close to the edge of the green to the hole.

Draw – A specialist shot where the ball curves from right to left in the air. The opposite of a fade.

Driver – The longest and least lofted club in the bag. Normally used for teeing off on par-4s or par-5s. Also referred to as the 1-wood.

Eagle – A score of two-under par on a hole.

Etiquette – An unwritten code of good behaviour which every golfer should follow.

Fade – A specialist shot where the ball curves from left to right in the air. The opposite of a draw.

Fairway – The area of closely mown grass on a golf course between the teeing area and the green.

Flyer – The term used to describe a shot which flies further than normal when blades of grass get trapped between the clubface and the ball.

Foursome – A match between two teams of two players. Each team has one ball and the players hit alternate shots.

Four-ball – A match between two teams of two players. Each player plays their own ball.

Fringe – The area of fairly short grass between the green and the fairway.

Front-nine – The first nine holes on an 18-hole course. Also referred to as the outward nine.

Follow-through – The final position in the swing.

Fore! – The word you should shout to warn other players on the course that a ball is heading towards them.

Green – The area of closely mown grass on a golf course, especially prepared for putting.

Grip – The term used for the way in which you hold the club and the leather or rubber part of the club which you place your hands on.

Gross score – Your total score before your handicap is deducted.

Grooves – Narrow ridges in the clubface designed to impart spin on the ball.

Handicap – The rating system which allows players of different standards to play competitively and an indication of a golfer's skill level.

Hole – The entire area of land between and including the teeing ground and the green, and also the ultimate target itself in the ground which is four and a quarter inches (10.8 cm) in diameter.

Honour – The right to tee off first on a hole. The honour is kept until another player beats your score on a hole.

Hook – A badly struck shot that travels sharply to the left when the ball leaves the clubface.

Hosel – The part of the golf club which connects the clubhead to the shaft.

Hickory – An old type of wood once used to manufacture golf shafts.

Impact – The point during the swing when the clubface strikes the ball.

Interlocking grip – A variation of the grip where the index finger on the left hand and the little finger on the right hand interlock.

Irons – Numbered one to sand wedge, the metal-headed clubs which are used to play shots from the tee, fairway and around the greens.

Knock-down shot – A shot that can be played against the wind or when you're in between clubs.

Late hit – The term used to describe the delayed unhinging of the wrists in the downswing, leading to extra power.

Lob shot – A specialist version of the chip shot which flies very high and stops quickly on the green.

Local knowledge – The term used to describe a golfer's familiarity with a golf course, usually their own home course.

Lie – The condition of the ground on which the ball comes to rest after hitting a shot.

Lie angle – The angle formed between the shaft and the ground.

Loft – The amount of elevation on the clubface measured between the top of the clubhead and the leading edge.

Matchplay – A format of competitive golf where you compete for holes. The winner is the person who wins the most holes during a round.

Medal play – A format of competitive golf where the player who takes the least number of strokes during a round wins. Also referred to as Strokeplay.

Mulligan – The term used to describe a second attempt at playing a shot, usually off the tee, and when the first shot wasn't very good. Not allowed in competitive golf.

Net – Your score at the end of the round after deducting your handicap from your gross total. See Gross.

Open stance – An address position where the feet and/or shoulders aim to the left of the target line. Opposite to closed stance.

Out of bounds – Normally highlighted by a series of white stakes, the area of the course which is outside the boundary lines. Golfers incur a penalty stroke and have to replay their shot again if their ball flies out of bounds.

Offset – A specific style of clubhead designed to help higher-handicap golfers, where the clubface is set back from the hosel.

Par – The term used to describe the number of shots an expert golfer should take to complete a hole and the full 18 holes.

Pitch – A lofted shot, normally played between 30 and 70 yards (27 and 64 metres) from the green.

Pitchmark – The indentation caused when the ball lands on the green after an approach shot

Posture – The angles you create with your upper and lower body at address.

Punch shot – Often used when playing into the wind, a shot which flies on a lower trajectory than normal.

Putt – Usually a fairly short shot played on the green with a putter where the ball rolls along the ground.

Putter – A club with very little loft designed to roll the ball along the ground on the green.

Relief – Permission to lift and drop the ball without penalty.

Rough – Areas of unmown grass on the edges of fairways and around the green which catch wayward shots.

Round – The completion of all 18 holes on a golf course.

Sand wedge – A golf club with an extra wide sole specially designed for bunker shots.

Square stance – When the alignment of the feet, hips and shoulders all aim parallel to the target line.

Shaft – The component of the golf club which connects the grip to the clubhead.

Sole – The base part of the clubface which sits on the ground at address.

Sweet spot – The exact spot in the centre of the clubface where maximum power is applied to the ball at impact.

Takeaway – The first move away from the ball in the backswing.

Target line – The line between the ball and your intended target.

Tee pegs – Small wooden or plastic implements upon which you place the ball before hitting a tee shot.

Tee shot – The first/opening shot from the teeing ground on any hole.

Vardon grip – Also known as the overlap, the most common grip on Tour, where the little finger on the right hand overlaps the index finger on the left. Named after the famous English golfer, Harry Vardon.

Waggle – A gentle movement backwards and forwards with the wrists designed to relax the muscles in the hands and arms before hitting a shot

Yips – A nervous and involuntary twitch of the hands or arms that prevents golfers from putting and chipping correctly

INDEX

ACKNOWLEDGEMENTS

Jacket pictures: OCTOPUS PUBLISHING GROUP/Mark Newcombe

All images OCTOPUS PUBLISHING GROUP/Mark Newcombe except:
GOLF MONTHLY/Mark Newcombe 62 Bottom Left, 62 Bottom Right, 63 Top Left, 63 Top Centre Left, 63 Top Centre Right, 63 Top Right, 63 Bottom Left, 63 Bottom Centre Left, 63 Bottom Centre Right, 63 Bottom Right, 57 Bottom Left.
VISIONS IN GOLF/Mark Newcombe 6, 12, 13, 16 left, 16 right, 16 Top Right, 16 Bottom, 18 Top Left, 18 Bottom, 19 Top Left, 19 Bottom Right, 21.